T0209351

Freedom From The Spirit Of Fear

Pastor Willie A. Winters, Jr.

WESTBOW
PRESS®
A DIVISION OF THOMAS NELSON
& ZONDERVAN

Copyright © 2023 Pastor Willie A. Winters, Jr.

All rights reserved. No part of this book may be used or reproduced by any means, graphic, electronic, or mechanical, including photocopying, recording, taping or by any information storage retrieval system without the written permission of the author except in the case of brief quotations embodied in critical articles and reviews.

This book is a work of non-fiction. Unless otherwise noted, the author and the publisher make no explicit guarantees as to the accuracy of the information contained in this book and in some cases, names of people and places have been altered to protect their privacy.

WestBow Press books may be ordered through booksellers or by contacting:

WestBow Press
A Division of Thomas Nelson & Zondervan
1663 Liberty Drive
Bloomington, IN 47403
www.westbowpress.com
844-714-3454

Because of the dynamic nature of the Internet, any web addresses or links contained in this book may have changed since publication and may no longer be valid. The views expressed in this work are solely those of the author and do not necessarily reflect the views of the publisher, and the publisher hereby disclaims any responsibility for them.

Any people depicted in stock imagery provided by Getty Images are models, and such images are being used for illustrative purposes only. Certain stock imagery © Getty Images.

Sketch showing Fear by Donald Winters; Gift box by Wilhelmina Brooks

Scripture taken from the King James Version of the Bible.

ISBN: 979-8-3850-0674-8 (sc)
ISBN: 979-8-3850-0675-5 (e)

Print information available on the last page.

WestBow Press rev. date: 12/18/2023

Contents

Acknowledgment

I would like to take this time to thank my Lord and Savior Jesus Christ for enabling my dear brother Willie Winters Jr., to write this mini book on different subjects. This book has impacted many readers and will assist you in your growth in Christ. I dedicate this masterpiece to my beloved brother Bill who died on his birthday April 18, 2022 Bill fought cancer and a life sentence in the state of Michigan. Willie served 37 years in prison, while in prison Willie began preaching and teaching the gospel of Jesus Christ. Minister Willie Winters ministered to any and everyone who would listen to the word of God. In every prison that Willie was transferred to, he shared the gospel of Jesus Christ. Correctional officers, nurses that cared for my brother and family and friends did get a chance to see the first print of the first edition. Willie added some of his personal expressions in this particular volume. My brother Willie has been and will always be an inspiration in my life. My dear mother and father, how I miss their preaching and teachings. I thank my God for the apostolic teaching of the baptisms and the receiving of the Holy Ghost. My parents raised my siblings and I, to walk upright before God we didn't always do the right thing or say the right things growing up into adulthood, But most of us are in our right place with the Lord Jesus as of now, because of our parents, my dear brother Bill and our pastors kept praying for us to come back to our first love which is in Jesus Christ. Enjoy the passion and writings of this book.

To my sister, Mrs. Wilhelmina Winters Brooks, who invested in printing up this book, and designed the first cover. To my mother and her husband, Mr. James & Mrs. Dolly Winters Crenshaw, who invested in making this vision into a reality. And to my son, Mr. William A. Winters III, who invested in this Work of God.

Also, to my father, Mr. Willie A. Winters Sr., who taught me according to the Word of God what it means to be a Christian and a man. And to my daughter, Miss Natalee Winters and my three granddaughters, who invested in this Work of God, and to the rest of my family who inspired me to write this book.

Also, to Mr. Kenneth and Mrs. Selena Smith, who invested and helped to complete this Work of God, and to faithful partners in this ministry. Chief Editor: Wilhelmina Brooks. Assistant editors: Willie Jackson, John Yang and Aqua Miller. These men have helped me beyond just editing; for example, Willie Jackson (nick named Chill). When I first got here, in this hospital ward I was in terrible pain, I received help with my preparation of food, going to the store and keeping my area clean I was told by the medical facility that I had suffered a stroke. I lost some of my ability to do the basics, these men made it possible for the excerpts that you will be reading to be added to this mini book. Thank-you all in Jesus' Mighty Name.

Preface

This book was written to help you during times of recession, depression, or even famine. It will show you how to recognize and perfect your gift. It will also help you to bring in the money and wealth that you and your family need. Why? Because no matter how bad the economy is locally, nationally, or globally, you will prosper despite its ups and downs. For the famines or recessions are nothing new. For example, there was a famine or recession during Abraham's day and then years later in Isaac, his son's day. (kjv) Genesis 12:9-10 and 26:1-2. God prospered them and He can prosper you too.

You might be thinking, "Yeah right! You don't know me or my situation!" No, I don't know you personally or your situation, but I do know Divine Principles and Spiritual Laws that govern money and wealth.

And no matter who you are or what your situation is they will work for you and change your life tremendously!

For what I'm about to teach you is stronger than Wall Street, the Federal Reserve (or the people that print paper money), or corrupt CEO's that steal the hard-earned money of their investors. Why? Because it's based on one of the simplest principles of this life:

Supply and Demand. In other words, your gift is the **supply** that will meet the **demands** of men and women. And this will bring in the money and the wealth you and your family will need, for all it takes is Godly skills to pay the bills.

Foreword

This book, "Freedom From the Spirit of Fear" is about the author who had always been (afraid), bound by fear. I realized that he thought he'll never have anything worth having, but God taught him that he needed 'Knowledge' to overcome this spirit of fear, that he wasn't born with. I'm proud to know that he is now free through Christ Jesus.

His mother, Evangelist, Doctor Dolly Coad-Crenshaw

***The writer of this book didn't just wake up one day and say, "I'm going to write a book based on fear; teachings, living in sin, and learning how to be led by the spirit of God. The writer of this book displays "How your gift will make room for you." This book is scripture-based and founded upon the Word of God. My mom told me that my brother was 3 years of age when he wanted to preach the gospel of Jesus Christ. In church service he asked our father could he preach in the service. Our father told Willie, if God uses him to preach, he will preach someday.

This book is based on life experiences that my brother Willie has experienced. I enjoyed this book and look forward to more writings that will instruct me on what the word of God says about me and my life. This book will bless you and your family.

Sister to Willie Winters, Evangelist Brooks

CHAPTER ONE

Freedom From The Spirit of Fear

"My understanding is" If you follow the word of God and believe it; it will make you fearless. You will not be afraid of anybody or anything or be afraid under any circumstances in the mighty name of Jesus. For you will learn to walk above fear. You will learn to walk by faith and not by sight. (kjv) II Corinthians 5:7 What Is Fear? There are two kinds of fear in the Bible; one is fear as far as reverence (or great respect) for God. (kjv) I Samuel 11:47. I have found out that there is the fear that comes from the devil or a spirit that makes men afraid because (kjv) II Timothy 1:7 says: "For God hath not given us (or believers) the spirit of fear; but of power, and of love, and of a sound mind." Fear is a spirit, and it comes from Satan's kingdom, and it is the number one way that he tries to paralyze us or stop us. But let's prove this by the word of God that fear is indeed a spirit. (kjv) Luke 1:65 says: "And fear came on all that dwelt round them: and all of these sayings were noised abroad throughout all the hill country of Judea."

You see when danger or something happens out of the ordinary; fear comes. It comes OUTWARD–<u>IN</u>WARD is the number one way that he tries to paralyze us or stop us. But let's prove this by the word of God that fear is indeed a spirit. Luke 1:65 says: "And fear <u>came on</u> all that (but) not <u>inward-outward</u>. So fear comes <u>upon</u> a person and Fear is a spirit, and it comes from Satan's kingdom, and it paralyzed them. (kjv) In Luke 8:26-37, Jesus cast the devil out of a man in the country of Gadarenes. "The whole multiple of the country of Gadarenes round about besought him (Jesus) to depart from them;

CHAPTER ONE

For they were TAKEN with great fear, and he went up into the ship and returned." The word taking in the Greek is "Sunecho" which means" To arrest as a prisoner, to afflict, perplex, constrain or stop."

What happened to the whole country of Gadarenes? Great fear came upon those people, for fear is a spirit, and when you realize this truth: that fear is a spirit; you will begin to become fearless. Why? Because through the Mighty Name of Jesus we have power over the spirit of fear!

WHERE DID FEAR COME FROM?

My thoughts are **Fear** began in the Garden of Eden when Adam and Eve sinned because before they sinned, they talked and walked with God. For they were made in the image of God, after his likeness, so Adam and Eve had the very nature of God. But when they sinned, they took on the nature of the devil ("in my opinion") which is a coward. For listen to what Adam said after he sinned, "And the Lord God called unto Adam, and said unto him, Where art thou? And he said, I heard thy voice in the garden, and I was afraid, because I was naked; and I hid myself." (Kjv) Genesis 3:9-10. So, you see that Adam took on the devil's nature which is a coward. Why? Because the definition of a coward is, "A person who lacks courage, especially, one who is shamefully unable to control (or get rid of) his fear and so shrinks from danger or trouble." Adam was hiding from God because his nature had **changed** to a coward's nature. Therefore, he didn't want to face trouble, responsibility, or judgment. But....

What Does Fear Do To A Believer's Life?

The spirit of fear <u>attracts</u> the very thing that a person fears the most. Just like a magnet to metal it pulls and causes to come to pass what the person is very afraid of.

Job learned this truth the hard way, for he said, "For my sighing (or my worrying) cometh before I eat, and my roaring's are poured out like the waters. For the <u>thing</u> which I greatly **FEARED** is <u>come upon me</u>, and that which I was afraid of is COME UNTO ME." (kjv) Job 3:24-25. I want you to notice two things: fear came upon him <u>first</u> **THEN** that which he was afraid of <u>came</u> unto him.

My understanding is, fear works just like faith works because fear is faith twisted or inverted. Or it's the flip side of the evil "twin" of faith. The big difference is - it will destroy you and not bless you, for fear steals, kills, and destroys because it's of the devil. (kjv) St. John 10:10.

Now the act of being fearful is <u>believing</u> that which you fear <u>will</u> come to pass. So, to fear is to <u>believe</u>, or else WHY are you so afraid? And the truth is (if) you just go by what to see and hear all the time, you will always be fearful.

But you shouldn't be moved by just what you see, hear, and especially by what you believe. Why? Because what you believe **determines** how you will **REACT** to any situation, and if you go just by what you see and hear all the time you will always be a fearful person. For your information is only based on what you can see, hear, imagine, or believe and that's not <u>ENOUGH</u> information.

For example, the Bible says, "Faith cometh by hearing and hearing by the word of God." Romans 10:17. But watch this closely: fear also cometh by hearing, and hearing by what the devil and your five senses are telling you. So, the bottom line is, what do <u>you</u> **believe**?

You see, as human beings, we will **always** believe in something. In my words, (if) you don't believe this, then you will believe that; for example, a person says," I don't believe in nothing!" But guess what? He <u>still</u> **BELIEVES** that he doesn't believe in anything! For no human being can get out of that act of believing, because we were created to believe. Since this is true, why not believe God's Word?

WHAT CAN BELIEVERS DO TO OVERCOME THE SPIRIT OF FEAR?

[STEP 1]

You must first put on the Breastplate (or armor) of Righteousness, and righteousness is being in right standing with God. Ephesians (kjv) 6:10-18. In other words, you have to do what's right in God's Eyes and get the sin out of your life and stop living for the devil and just for yourself. And STOP feeding on the things of this world like disaster movies that tell you that this will happen to the Earth in the future, so be afraid be very afraid. Or news programs that tell you-you better be afraid because this happens locally or nationally, or internationally. Or scary movies that make millions of dollars on creative ways to make you afraid. For people say when they're looking for a good scary movie, "How was the movie?" The other person says, "Oh it was really good because it scared me to death!

5

[Step 2]

You need to understand that your heart is either filled with faith or its filled with fear. For whatever you have been constantly feeding into your spirit or heart is exactly what will eventually be produced in your life. (KJV version) Proverbs 4:23 "Keep thy heart with <u>all</u> diligence (or guard what goes in it); for out of <u>it</u> are the issues (or the building blocks) of life (whether good or evil)."

Therefore, if you don't spend a lot of time in the Word of God you will be filled with fear. Why? Because something has to fill up the empty space in your heart and it doesn't matter whether it's fear or faith. Now faith cometh by constantly hearing, and hearing by the Word of God.

This is extremely important because faith in God's Word is the <u>only thing</u> that has the power to drive out the spirit of fear completely out of your heart and keep it out.

But when you feed on fear words and fear thoughts like," I'm afraid I'm going to catch something and get sick! Or I'm scared that they might lay me off! Or I don't believe I'm going to make it because gas and food prices are too high!"

These are fear words and fear thoughts, and (if) you keep saying them or thinking them, you will bring them to pass in your life, because you <u>believe</u> every thought and every word you said. (kjv) Mark 11:22-23.

My understanding is The Word of God and doing it is the only thing that will keep you out of fear. So, you have to study to show yourself approved unto God. (kjv) II Timothy 2:15. And you must desire the sincere milk of the Word that you may **grow thereby**. (kjv) 1st Peter 2:2.

We the saints of God must also **do** the Word, and you must practice it in everyday circumstances and not just on Sunday or around other Christians. Because you must constantly practice the Word of The Living God daily, for talk is cheap, so if you're going to talk it – walk it.

You see my brother or sister; you have to study and feed on the Word of God **every day** to get all that fear out of your heart and keep it out. Study the scriptures and make them a part of your daily life. In other words, you should spend so much time with them until you can quote them by heart and not from the head. For memorization or just from the mind works, but in extreme or dangerous situations, our minds tend to shut off on us.

But our spirit man, the inner man, or the hidden man of the heart will rise to extreme or dangerous situations.

And the thought came to me, the writer Ephesians 3:16 & 1st Peter 3:3,4 (kjv version). Because he has the Word rooted and grounded in him, but if you haven't spent enough time in the Word, you will not have the spiritual strength or power to override the spirit of fear, because you're too weak; for example, like the man who spends all of his time watching TV on the couch, and over time he has developed a beer gut that makes him look like he's 9 months pregnant! Suddenly his front door is kicked open! And this muscle-bound dude storms into his living room and says, "I'm taking your wife, your kids, and your house over, and if you try to stop me, I will kill you!"

What can the fat man do? He's too fat to quickly run and get a weapon, so he can't do NOTHING! He's out of shape and helpless, and he has no muscle power to stop this dangerous predator. Why?

Because he hasn't been spending time working out or building his muscles.

You see, we eat natural food to have the strength to move things or to work. This is also true concerning spiritual food or faith food, for as you feed on the Word of God, you're building up and stirring up strength; strength to overcome the spirit of fear. The scriptures listed are taken from the (kjv version) Therefore, start working out spiritually right now by looking up these important scriptures and studying them.

II Timothy 1:7	Luke 10:19	1st John 4:18
Psalms 91	1st John 5:18	James 4:7
Psalms 23	Isaiah 54: 14-17	Joshua 1:5-9
Psalms 103: 20	Acts 16: 16-18	Ephesians 6:10-18

[STEP 3]

My thoughts are since fear is a spirit, we are not dealing with something natural, but supernatural. Therefore, we MUST use supernatural weapons to deal with them. The Word says, "For though we walk in the flesh, we (Christians) do not war after the flesh: For the weapons of our warfare are not carnal (or man-made), but mighty (or supernatural) through God to the pulling down of strongholds;" (kjv) II Corinthians 10:3-4.

And the thought came to me, we wrestle **NOT** against flesh and blood, but against spirits. (kjv) Ephesians 6:12. Therefore, you must take authority of the spirit of fear in the Name of Jesus. The Bible says, "Submit yourselves therefore to God. **RESIST** the devil, and he will flee (as in terror) from you." (kjv) James 4:7. My understanding of what Jesus was teaching his disciples and us is, **YOU** must do this and **NOT** God, for He has done all He's going to do about the devil. We as saints of the Most High must resist him (the devil) In the Mighty Name of Jesus.

My interpretation is Either you do it or it won't get done, and if for any reason you choose not to do it, the devil **DOESN'T** have to flee (if) you don't **RESIST** him because it's according to the legality or inflexibility of the Word of God. And that rat knows God's Word, so he will say to God, "He didn't resist me - so I don't have to flee from him!" Because God gave us power over the devil, for the Bible says, "And the seventy (disciples of Jesus) return with joy, saying, Lord, even the devils are subject unto us **THROUGH THY NAME.** And he said unto them, I beheld Satan as lightning fall from heaven. Behold, I give unto you **POWER** to tread on serpents and scorpions (or evil spirits), and **OVERALL,** the power of the enemy (or the devil): and nothing shall by any means hurt you (kjv Luke 10:19).

NOTWITHSTANDING in this rejoice not, that the spirits are subject unto you; but rather rejoice, **BECAUSE** your names are written in heaven (or that you all are children of God)." (kjv) Luke 10:17-20.

My interpretation of what Jesus was teaching His disciples and us is, every believer has power over all the power of the devil. But why is this true? It's true because Satan and every devil in hades are subject to every believer that is born again <u>and</u> **BELIEVES** in the power of the Mighty Name of Jesus. For the Bible says, Jesus' Name is, "**FAR ABOVE ALL PRINCIPALITY,** and power, and might, and dominion, and **every** name that is named, not only in this world, but also in that which is to come:" (kjv) Ephesians 1:21.

You see, there is great power in the Name of Jesus (but) **YOU** must believe in that Name. The Bible also says, "And his **NAME** through **FAITH IN HIS NAME** hath **MADE** this man strong…" (kjv) Acts 3:16. When you believe in the Name of Jesus and rebuke (or tell it to go away from you) the spirit of fear will flee from you because it fears the Name of Jesus. So, keep rebuking it with authority (or with anger) until it leaves you, or fight the good fight of faith. (kjv) 1ˢᵗ Timothy 6:12. For the devil fears the Name of Jesus, because Jesus defeated Satan and whipped him very badly in his kingdom, for the Bible says, "And having spoiled (or ruined) principalities and powers, he (Jesus) made a shew of them (the devil and his demons) OPENLY, triumphing OVER THEM in it (or Satan's kingdom)." (kjv) Colossians 2:15. Jesus also said, "I am he that liveth, and was dead; and, behold, I am alive for evermore, Amen; and have the keys of hell and death." (kjv) Revelation 1:18.

[STEP 4]

My thoughts, Believe the Word of God instead of what you see or how you feel. In other words, take God at His Word, because you must believe WHAT the Word says; for example, God through His Word promises us divine protection. He promises to protect us by His holy angels and there are different types of angels, and they are very real.

Some Angels just deliver messages like Gabriel, and then there are Angels of war, like Michael whose job is to protect the body of Christ, and they're the best protectors in the world. You can't see them with your natural eye, but they are there, nonetheless. For the Word says that they are there, and by FAITH we know they are here with us.

(kjv) Psalms 103:20 says, "Bless the Lord, ye his angels, that excel in strength, that do his commandments (or the Word of God), hearkening (or doing) unto the voice of his Word."

If you are speaking or doing things against the Word, your Angels are kept from protecting you completely or they can't protect you at all. Why? Because they OBEY the voice of His Word. So you have to speak the Word or speak scriptures concerning your circumstances, and NOT speak fear words. Why?

For your Angels are **LISTENING TO YOU** and they go by the Word of God **ONLY,** but they will protect you 100% (if) you do and speak the Word of God concerning your situation. This is very important because just **one angel** killed 185,000 soldiers in one night. II Kings 19:35. Now, this was just one of them but imagine what two or four of them could do to keep you and your family safe.

In steps 1, 2, 3, & 4 we covered how to put yourself in a position to get rid of the spirit of fear, and how to rebuke the spirit of fear in the Mighty Name of Jesus. But there is another way to overcome fear even after you have done all of this; for example, two little boys were playing in a neighbor's backyard. One of the little boys was from out of town and the other one lived right next door. But there was a big vicious dog chained to a tree in this same backyard where they were secretly playing.

When the dog realized they were there, he started barking and violently charged at the two playing boys. And as the dog was charging at them, the boy from out of town jumped and ran as fast as he could to get away!

But the boy that lived next door stood his ground and didn't run, neither was he afraid of the charging dog. For suddenly just as the dog came a few feet from where he was standing, his long chain came to a quick end!! And it jerked the charging dog back and he fell to the ground! The other little boy that ran in fear came back to his friend and said, "Why didn't you run?! Why were you not afraid of the dog?!"

The boy who lived next door smiled really big and showed two of his fingers and tapped his temple and said, **"KNOWLEDGE!** I knew how **LONG** the chain was, but that brainless dog must have forgotten!"

You see, the secret to fearlessness is also **KNOWLEDGE** of God's Word: His Angels and His ability to protect us by knowing our past, our present situation, and our future. This helps us not to be afraid, for David said, "Yea, though I walk through the valley of the shadow of death, I will **FEAR NO EVIL;** for (or this is the reason) thou art with me: thy **ROD** and thy **STAFF** they comfort me." (kjv) Psalms 23:4. A Shepherd's rod is a long piece of wood with a bit hook on one end. In other words, the reason why this comforted David was because the rod part is an offensive weapon to fight off wolves, in the staff part (or hook) is a defensive tool to grab a lost or hurt sheep that's trapped on the side of a mountain.

In my opinion David knew this first hand because he used to be a shepherd. Therefore, knowledge gets rid of fear: the knowledge of knowing that God Almighty is protecting you and your family. Plus, faith in God's promises of divine protection, and believing **MORE IN THEM** than in the devil's ability to hurt you is what works.

But fear is having faith in the devil's ability to hurt you, or in the evil circumstances that threaten to destroy you.

And this is why the first thing according to the Holy Bible, an angel would say when he appeared to individuals in the Bible was, "Fear Not!" (kjv) Luke 1:11-13. Why? Because you can't operate in fear and faith at the **SAME** time! So, it's interesting to see that the words **FEAR NOT** appears more than 60 times in the Bible, because it's a serious problem with God's people. But knowledge of God's Word will make a man, a woman, or even a child utterly fearless.

[STEP 5]

You must practice all of these steps every day, or every time fear tries to come on you. So, let's recap on these steps: step one; stay in right standing with God or put on the breastplate of righteousness.

Step two; be full of the Word of God, for faith cometh by hearing and hearing by the Word of God. Because faith or being full of faith destroys the spirit of fear.

Step three; learn to bind Satan and rebuke the spirit of fear in the Mighty Name of Jesus. For it reminds him of his total and hurtful defeat at Calvary, and there are powerful Angels standing by to force the spirit of fear to obey you. Plus, fear is a spirit, so it's **ALWAYS** subject to or **MUST BOW TO** the Mighty Name of Jesus!

[STEP 6]

Since we are dealing with supernatural beings, we must use the Powerful Name of Jesus as our **WEAPON.** For pleading the Blood of Jesus will not make the devil run from you, no, it's the Name of Jesus that he fears the most and not the Blood. The Bible does say that they overcame him by the Blood of the Lamb and the word of their testimony, but this is talking about being cleansed from sin and it makes death pass over you. (kjv) Romans 3:24, 25, Ephesians 1:3-7, Hebrews 9:11-22 & Exodus 12:12-13. So that precious Blood did give us total victory over the devil concerning sin and death. (kjv)

Revelation 12:11. But you must take authority over the spirit of fear in the Mighty Name of Jesus.

The last step is five, which is to believe what the Word says instead of what the devil says, or what your circumstances are saying to you by their **mere** existence. Also, you must have Bible knowledge or working knowledge of God's Word concerning divine protection. This includes believing in the outward working of God's powerful Angels, for He has given them charge over you to protect you and your family.

But you must **PRACTICE** these steps every day, everywhere, and every time you are faced with a difficult or dangerous situation. Why? Because being fearless will not come to you overnight, but it will come by continually practicing the Word, meditating (or thinking or pondering deeply) on God's promises and speaking the Word out of your mouth. And one day you'll wake up and there will be no fear in your heart, for something dangerous will suddenly happen around you or to you, but you would not be afraid; for example, one time I was watching a movie with some people and a lion suddenly jumped out of a bush right at us! Everyone sitting around me jumped out of fear, but I didn't. Why? There was no fear in me, faith had replaced the fear that was once in my heart.

Faith will make you and keep you strong, and you will also be of good courage. Joshua 1:6. I reference Psalms 23; Yea, though you walk through the valley of the shadow of death, you will **FEAR NO EVIL: f**or God is with you, His rod and His staff they comfort you. Therefore, you are more than a conqueror through the power of the Mighty Name of Jesus! And you are an overcomer and not a fearful person or a coward, for the Bible says:

He that overcometh shall inherit all things; and I will be his God, and he shall be my son. **BUT** the **FEARFUL,** and unbelieving, and the abominable, and murderers, and whoremongers, and sorcerers, and idolaters, and all liars, shall have **THEIR PART** in the lake which burneth with fire and brimstone: which is the second death. (kjv) Revelation 21:7-8

I want you to notice that God puts the fearful or "Cowards" right alongside whoremongers, sorcerers, and murderers. Why? Because God **HATES FEAR!!** For people have gone to hades because of a cowardly Christian:

a person who was afraid to witness to people and tell them the truth about Jesus Christ.

Fear or, being fearful will not only cause a person to lose the blessing of God in their lives, but it can also cause a person to DENY Jesus under great persecution, pressure, or the fear of being tortured or put to death for their belief.

And this happens a lot in Godless countries or a simple situation like when Peter denied Jesus in the company of His enemies. (kjv) Mark 14:66-72. But it's very important that you understand how serious this is, for Jesus said, "Whosoever therefore shall confess me before men (or in their company), him will I confess also before my Father which is in heaven. But whosoever shall DENY me before men (or in their company), him will I ALSO DENY before my Father which is in heaven." (kjv) Matthew 10:32-33.

Jesus is saying that a person's cowardice actions could cause them to go to hades! So a person could spend eternity in the lake of fire and brimstone because they were afraid to stand up for Jesus under any circumstances.

You see, fear is of the devil, so you must resist it in the Mighty Name of Jesus every time it comes upon you. You have to say out now or under your breath, if people are around you, "Satan I bind you in the Mighty Name of Jesus! Spirit of fear, I rebuke you in Jesus' Mighty Name!"

Then pray and ask for God's strength, and that His peace would come upon you in Jesus' Name. For binding Satan works, because when you bind him (the devil), Angels surround him and make him stop what he's doing or trying to do to you. Plus, Jesus said, "Verily I say unto you, Whatsoever ye shall BIND on earth shall be bound in heaven: and whatsoever ye shall loose on earth shall be loosed in heaven." (kjv) Matthew 18:18. He also said, "No man can enter into a strong man's house (or kingdom), and spoil his goods, except he will FIRST BIND the strong man; and THEN he will spoil his house." (kjv) Mark 3:27. Therefore, learn to bind Satan when you are dealing with the spirit of fear and when you are faced with very difficult or dangerous situations. Bind Satan first and then rebuke the spirit of fear, for now, you have cut off its power source. You should do this, EVERY TIME you become afraid so that it becomes a habit. In other words, you react instead of acting because it has become a habit to you. And you CAN DO THIS because you are a child of God, and He has given you His courage and ability. But you must act, for the Word says, "Submit yourselves therefore to God. RESIST THE DEVIL, and he will flee from YOU." (kjv) James 4:7.

Also, the Word says that you can do all things through Christ (or His anointing) which strengthens you. (kjv) Philippians 4:13.

Now pray this prayer with me if you are a Christian (but) if you're not, I have a prayer for you to: "Father, I come to you in the Mighty Name of Jesus. Forgive me for being afraid, forgive me for every time I wouldn't stand up for you. I ask you to strengthen me with power and might in my inner man by the Holy Spirit according to (kjv) Ephesians 3:16 and give me a holy boldness. I ask you to make me strong and of good courage, and to help me speak boldly as I ought to speak. Lord, help me to become bold and fearless, and I ask you to let your peace come upon me. Give me peace of mind about this situation I'm facing. I ask these things from you in Jesus' Mighty Name, Amen."

Since you have prayed this with me, I want you to start learning how to resist the spirit of fear, so say out loud and with authority or with anger," Satan! I bind you in the Mighty Name of Jesus! Spirit of fear, I command you to come out of my heart in the Mighty Name of Jesus!"

Now if you don't know God, pray this prayer with me: "Dear God, I'm a sinner, but I believe that Jesus Christ died for my sins and rose from the grave. And on the strength of this, I ask you to forgive me for every sin I've ever committed and I'm sorry for my sins. Lord Jesus, come into my heart and take control of my life. For you said in your Word that if I believe in my heart that you died for my sins and rose from the grave and that if I confess you with my mouth by asking you to come into my heart, I will be saved according to Romans 10:8-10. I believe Lord Jesus, so I also ask you to fill me with your Holy Spirit and I will speak in other tongues by faith in Jesus Mighty Name according to (kjv) Luke 11:9-13 & Mark 16:16-18. A-men."

Now begin to worship God by saying, Thank-you Jesus, thank-you Jesus! Hallelujah, hallelujah, hallelujah!" Now any syllables that are not your native tongue, start speaking them by faith. For the Holy Spirit will help you as you start speaking some syllables by faith. And it might sound like gibberish (but) speak them anyway, for if you do this every day with your regular praying, it will become more fluent. (kjv) Acts 2:4.

Now if you practice the Word every day, you will become fearless, but you still need to check up on yourself every few months. Why? Because over time fear can creep back into your heart. But how do you do this?

Simple, if something unexpected or dangerous happens to you or around you. See if fear comes upon you, or you feel fearful in your heart because of the danger or the suddenness of something happening to you. If it didn't, you're still full of faith.

But if it did, fear has secretly quietly crept back into your heart. So, you need to diligently get back into the Word of God and repeat all of this that you have learned in this book.

Now immediately get all of that fear out of your heart - don't waste another minute. Get that fear out of you, and then make up your mind and settle it in your heart forever that you are going to live fearlessly; no matter who, what, or where. Because fearlessness takes staying in right standing with God and staying constantly in His Word, for The Word says, "Thou wilt KEEP HIM in perfect peace, whose MIND IS STAYED ON THEE: because he trusteth in thee (or he believes the Word, and walks by faith and not by sight)." Isaiah 26:3

You see, your faith in God's Word will keep you in perfect peace and keeping your mind on God's Word instead of your evil circumstances - will keep you fearless. The Word of God will comfort your heart and mind IF you believe it and act on it.

But what is faith? Faith is believing God's Word and then acting on it. Even so, faith, if it hath NOT WORKS, is DEAD, being alone. Yea, a man may say, Thou hast faith, and I have works: shew me thy faith without thy works, and I will shew thee my faith BY MY WORKS. Seest thou how faith wrought (or worked) with his works, and By Works was faith Made Perfect?

(Or complete where it works for you) (kjv) James 2:17-18 22.

Therefore, faith without works or corresponding actions is dead, or ineffective; for example, concrete mix (still in powder form) is useless without adding water to it. So, you must act on God's Word to get results, and remember: For God hath NOT given US the SPIRIT of fear; but of power, and of love, and of a sound mind. (kjv) II Timothy 1:7.

CHAPTER TWO

The Gift

You have a gift, a talent, a purpose that was put in your heart from birth, for the Bible says, "Then the word of the Lord came unto me (Jeremiah) saying, <u>Before </u>I (God) formed thee in the belly I knew thee, and <u>before</u> thou camest forth out of the womb I sanctified thee (or set you apart for a specific purpose), and I ordained thee a prophet unto the nations." (kjv) Jeremiah 1: 4,5.

God told Jeremiah that He placed in his heart from birth his gift or his purpose before he was even born; for example, when I was four years old I would sit on my father's lap during services in his church. And I would beg my father to let me preach. I would say, "Daddy, daddy! Let me preach! Please, daddy let me preach!"

At first, he thought that I just wanted to be like him, but then one service I said the same things (but) this time with more seriousness. He looked at me with a puzzled look on his face as if he was seeing something different about me.

So, he said, "I'm going to let you preach and you **better** preach!"

I jumped down and went in front of the congregation and said, "The Holy Ghost is the truth, preach the Holy Ghost!" And when I was saying these things, I felt something come over me (it was the anointing to preach), but then I started pointing to different members of the congregation and telling them that they were living the wrong way and it lifted off me. My daddy immediately came and picked me up and brought me back to the pulpit.

You see, sometimes God starts dealing with a person when they are still a child concerning their gift, and those times will stay with them for the rest of their lives; for example, God started dealing with Samuel the prophet and with Samson this way while they were very young. (kjv) I Samuel 1: 9-28, and (kjv) Judges 13:24-25.

In my own opinion the gift inside of each of us is a gift / a piece of God or He took your gift out of His being; for example, the Bible says when talking about life and death, "Then shall the dust (or our bodies) return to the earth as it was: and the **spirit** shall return unto God <u>who gave it</u>." (kjv) Ecclesiastes 12:7. So when we die our spirits return to God who gave them to us in the first place and this is why everyone must stand before God or return to Him for judgment because that which came out of God <u>must</u> return to him (my opinion the writer).

For we came out of God and entered a physical body, and this is why babies are so pure or they have an aura of purity about them when they're born because they haven't committed any sins. And this is also why babies or young children when they die under the age of 12, which is the age of accountability, go directly to heaven. For God is a Spirit and He created all spirits, and this is also true concerning our gifts they come directly from God. (kjv) St. John 4: 24.

You see my brother or sister; your gift or gifts are put on this earth to solve problems that plague mankind. For when God wants to help someone, He sends a man or a woman to that person, because inside of them is the gift or the <u>answer</u> to their problems. But why is this important to you today?

It's important because your service to God and man is tied to your gift or what God created for you to do for Him, or this is the way He wants you to personally benefit mankind.

This is true, but your gift will also give you the **direction** your life should take; for example, the Bible says, "Where there is <u>no vision</u>, the people <u>perish</u>: but he that keepeth the law (or the Word of God), happy is he." (kjv) Proverbs 29:18

The word "Vision" means, "Assignment, a mission or a dream to fulfill or a revelation or an oracle He wants you to teach others, or a command directly from God telling you to do something." Therefore, where there is no vision the people perish. Why? Because they have nothing to strengthen them or give them hope during hard times, so they have no direction in their lives.

And this is why most people fail in this life, for they have no vision, so they're driving their lives just like their car at night without the headlights being on.

For you have to **know** or see where you're going, because if you don't at least know where you're going – you won't know when you get there. Plus, without a vision, you also don't know who to let in your life and who not to let in your life. Or what to do with your money and what not to do with your money. Who to marry and who not to marry. Who's an asset and who's a liability? Who will help you reach your goals and who will hinder you or even stop you from reaching your goals. In other words, when you know **where** you're going; you can figure out exactly what it will take to get there. This is why vision or knowing your gift is so important, for it dictates who, what, when, and where.

For you were put on this earth to help others, even (if) you don't understand it right now; for example, when I was in the first grade they let us out for recess, so we all went to the playground to play. But in the middle of the playground, there was this little boy on one knee working hard to untie a knot in his shoe. I looked at him struggling and knew I could help him because I had learned the secret to untying knots by playing with them. So I said, "Hey, let me help you with that because I'm good at untying knots!" In seconds I had the knot untied and he ran away happy.

But this little girl who was watching us came over with tears coming down her cheeks and without saying a word, stuck her shoe out with a knot in it towards me. So, I bent down and untied her knot too. She wiped her tears away and laughed and then ran away happy! I didn't understand it then, but I just knew in my heart that I should help people with problems they can't solve by themselves. And guess what? You can too! But how?

UNDERSTANDING GOD'S PURPOSES FOR A GIFT

My understanding and opinion is for any gift that God gives a person has three specific purposes: **First** what God created you to do for Him or you're His Hands in the earth; for example, giving to the poor, (kjv) Proverbs 19:17 or being in law enforcement or the military service. (kjv) Romans 13:1-4. Or being a mother or a father. (kjv) Ephesians 6:1-4. Or a politician such as a governor or a president, or a king or queen.

(kjv) Daniel 4:17. For the Bible says, "Every good gift (or even secular gifts) and every perfect gift (or spiritual gifts such as teaching or preaching God's word, or singing or any ministerial things for God) is from above, and cometh down from the Father of Lights (or the God of inspiration) with whom is no variableness, neither shadow of turning (nor He doesn't change)." (kjv) James 1:17. Therefore whatever your gift is, it will directly or indirectly further God's plan of Redemption for mankind.

The **second** area of purpose for a gift is to directly serve or benefit mankind either locally, nationally, or globally.

And your service will be in such a way that **only you** can do it most effectively. Why? Because you are unique, so much so there is only (1) of you in the whole universe.

The definition of unique is, "One and only, having no like or equal; unparalleled." Because God created you in such a way, there is only (1) of you in existence.

Therefore, only you can do the best job or use that gift properly. In other words, when it comes to doing what God called you to do – you have no competition. You have no equal. Why because?

"No one can beat you at being you!" For your style is innate, or it's the **essence** of you.

And this is why God needs you to fulfill what He called you to do; for example, many people say to their friends when they see them doing something they don't like, "If I were you, I would do that a lot differently!"

I will never forget the true story that I heard about a minister who was very frustrated about doing a job that he believed God told him to do. He said, "God! I can't do this!! I keep getting things wrong!" I was told, the young minister heard the Lord speak to his (spirit man) with the words "Don't worry about it, for you were my third choice to do that job. For I called a man to do it but he wouldn't obey me, so I am using you to do what he could have done with less effort. Do the best you can, and I will give you his reward."

This is deep, because it appears that the young minister was the third choice." In other words, some things the Lord may not tell us (the saints of God) to do a particular thing in the first place (but) he may still need the job to be done by someone else my personal opinion is that the Lord will give you the ability to do what he asked you to do." Or as the parable says, take the talent from him that was wicked, slothful, and disobedient and give it to the person who has 10 talents. Or give it to the one who uses his gifts. (kjv) Matthew 25: 14-28.

You see my brother or sister when a person refuses to do what God called them to do or refuses to use their gift, He's forced to use someone else, and it will be difficult for them to do what would have been a lot easier for the person who was God's first choice. The third area is, your money and wealth are tied directly to your gift. Now you can do this or that in this life, but these things will not even come close to producing the money and wealth your gift will produce for you. Why?

Because there are money and wealth assigned to come to the gift that God has personally placed in your heart. Or there is money and wealth that He has already commanded to come to you (if) you use your gift for His purposes.

And this money and wealth are so attached to your gift until even if you don't use it for God, it will still bring in money and wealth; for example, many famous singers started in the church, but later went to the world with their gift and became rich (but they will pay for this, for God is not mocked or He will not tolerate being treated like a fool. Galatians 6:2. So, it doesn't matter what the economy is doing or what it isn't doing, because your money and wealth have already been assigned to come to you, but why?

THERE IS ASSIGNED MONEY AND WEALTH

I'm going to prove to you by the scriptures that **your** money and wealth are directly attached to your gift. For God created you and He knows you inside and out, so in His infinite wisdom, He has already assigned these things to come to you when you **activate** your gift. Why? Because He's smart enough to realize that if there is something in it for you to fulfill His purposes – you will do them. And this is where I got the term "Assigned Money and Wealth."

Now to prove this, let's start with ministers as our first example, because winning the lost and teaching the Body of Christ is God's **first** priority, for the Bible says, "Who goeth a warfare anytime at his own charges (or at his expenses)? who planteth a vineyard, and eateth not of the fruit thereof? Or who feedeth a flock, and eateth not of the milk of the flock? Say I these things as a man (or some sort of con job)? or saith, not the law (or the Word of God) the same also? For it is written in the Law of Moses, Thou shalt not muzzle the mouth of the ox that treadeth out the corn. Doth God take care for oxen (or is He only saying this to make sure the oxen get fed)? Or saith he altogether for our sakes (or to give us a physical example to explain a spiritual truth)?

For our sakes, no doubt, this is written: that he that ploweth (or works for God) should plow in hope (or expect to receive a reward); and he that thresheth in hope should be partaker of his hope (by using his gift). If we have sown unto you spiritual things (by using our gifts), is it a great (or terrible) thing if we shall reap your carnal things (or your money and wealth)?

Now starting at verse (kjv) 1st Corin 9:13, it says, "Do ye not know that they (or ministers) which minister about holy things live (or receive their money and wealth) of the things of the temple, (or the church)? And they which wait (or attend) at the altar are partakers with the altar (or they receive some of the things offered on the altar)? Even so, hath the Lord ordained (or made it a Spiritual Law) that they which preach the gospel should live (or get their money and wealth) of the gospel." (kjv) I Corinthians 9: 7-14.

You see my brother or sister, a minister's money and wealth comes directly from his gift. God Almighty made it a Spiritual Law or ordained it this way so that they which preach the gospel shall get their livelihood directly from the gospel.

In my reading of the Holy Bible and understanding, I now know that the greatest minister that ever walked this earth was Jesus Christ, so He's our Highest example. Did He receive money and wealth from people by His gifts? The Bible says, "And it came to pass afterward, that He (Jesus) went through every city and village, preaching and showing the glad tidings (or Good News) of the Kingdom of God: and the twelve were with Him, and <u>certain women</u>, which had been **healed** of evil spirits and infirmities, Mary called Magdalene, out of whom went seven devils, And Joanna the wife of Chuza Herod's steward, and Susanna, and <u>many</u> <u>others</u>, which ministered (or gave) unto him of their <u>substance</u>." (kjv) Luke 8:1-3

According to Strong's Concordance, the Greek word for "Substance" in the New Testament is the word for hupostasis. The New Testament Greek word "Huparchonta" which means, "Property, wealth, goods or substance." Therefore, Jesus received money and wealth from the people as He ministered to them by His gifts.

You see, most religious people believe that Jesus and His disciples floated on a White Cloud from city to city to preach the gospel. No! Jesus' ministry was real and to maintain it, He received money and wealth from the people He ministered to with His gifts. But a good example of receiving money and wealth during a crisis is the Apostle Paul, who at the time was shipwrecked, for the Bible says, "And when they were escaped (from the sea), then they knew that the island was called Melita. And the barbarous people showed us no little kindness (or a lot of kindness): for they kindled a fire, and received us every one, because of the present rain, and because of the cold." (kjv) Acts 28:1-2.

Now let's go down in the same chapter to verse 7, "In the same quarters were possessions of the chief man of the island, whose name was Publius; who received us, and lodged us three days courteously. And it came to pass, that the father of Publius lay sick of a fever and a bloody flux: to whom Paul entered in, and prayed, and laid his hands on him, and healed him. So when this was done, **others also,** which had diseases in the island, came, and were healed: Who also (or with the chief of the island) honored us with many honors (or with money and wealth); and when we departed, they laded us (or loaded us down) with such things as were necessary." (kjv) Acts 28:7-10.

The word "Honored" in Strong's Concordance the original Greek writings of the New Testament is, "Ti-me" which means, "Money paid or valuables." So, Paul's ministry of healing brought him money and wealth in a place where he had nothing but the clothes on his back! For he was shipwrecked and couldn't even speak their language (but) with the gift that God had placed in his life, he communicated help or solved their problems.

But how do I know this? The Bible said that they were barbarous people and if you study these verses carefully, you will notice that there wasn't a word spoken between Paul and them during the entire time he was there. Why? Because a gift is **greater** than language barriers or race, or even poverty that's so terrible that you don't have anything, and you can't see any way of getting anything. But how is this possible?

YOUR GIFT WILL MAKE ROOM FOR YOU

The word "Gift" in the original Hebrew writings of the Old Testament is "Mattan" which means, "A present or a gift to give." So, your gift was given to you by God to give away to others. And when you give it to others, you are giving them a piece of God. This is why seeing it or hearing it can move us to tears.

A person asked me one time after I finished teaching on this subject," But how do you know if what you are seeing, or hearing is a gift?" I said, "You know it when you can't do it!"

Now the word "Room" in Hebrew is "Raw-khab" which means, "To broaden, or make room, or to force open." Your gift will **force open** a way for you or make a way when there is no way. In other words, you might find yourself in a situation like the Apostle Paul, who had nothing left but the wet shirt on his back.

And like him, it looks like you don't have anything to work with either, yet your bills are past due, and more are piling up every day. Or you're about to lose your job, apartment, or house, or you have already lost these things. But believe it or not, you do have something of great value in your heart: a present that God gave you at birth. And if you start right now seeking His Face by fasting, prayer and studying His written Word, He will reveal to you your gift, for He said, "And ye shall seek me, and find me, **When** ye shall search for me with all your heart." (kjv) Jeremiah 29:13. So God has promised you that (if) you seek Him with all your heart, you will find Him or He will give you the knowledge of your gift.

This is one way to find out what your gift is, but there are other ways because Jesus said, "For where your treasure is, there will your heart be also." (kjv) Matthew 6:21.

Let's flip this scripture over and it will read, "For where your heart is, **there** will your treasure be also." In other words, what's **burning** in your heart, or what's your passion? What moves you to great anger or great joy? Or what jobs or hobbies you're not only willing to do them (but) you like them so much, until you would pay people to let you do them!

For example, years ago I had preached hundreds of sermons

before I received a tithe or an offering. So when members started tithing to my ministry, I laughed because I would have preached to them for free!

Godly passions are strong indicators of your gift or what you're supposed to be doing; for example, Jesus' Passion was going to the cross for our sins. (kjv) Acts 1:1-3. For where your passion is, there will be your treasure also. Whether its music or teaching something to others or helping people in a certain area or building things. Whatever it is, it's something that greatly moves you and you also like watching other people do it.

The Bible says, "Having then gifts differing according to the grace (or power of God), that is given to us, whether prophecy, (or speaking for God as God uses the vessel), let us prophesy according to the proportion of faith; Or ministry (which covers many areas: pastors, deacons, ushers or children's ministry or any official service), let us wait on our ministering (or on God's Timing and not on our timing): or he that teacheth (or has a teaching ministry or a Sunday school teacher, so wait), on teaching. Or he that exhorteth (or using consolation by uplifting others, or to entreat them to do something good or something the right way, or to give them a warning, so wait), on exhortation: he that giveth (or give to others by sharing their money and wealth, or philanthropy), let him do it with simplicity (or with sincerity and not for your glory. (kjv) Matthew 6:1-4); he that ruleth (or presides over anything), with diligence (or in earnestness, or take God's Business very seriously. (kjv) Acts 6:1-3) he that sheweth mercy (or to be compassionate by God's Divine Grace by helping the homeless, the down and out or the forgotten men and women in prison), with cheerfulness (or be nice even when they don't appreciate it or have a very nasty attitude towards you)."

(kjv) Romans 12:6-8. These are some of the gifts that God gives to the body of Christ. But what is your gift?

YOUR GIFT

We have covered spiritual gifts that are outlined in (kjv) Romans 12:6-8, and some secular gifts to see which one fits you, and now we're going to cover some more spiritual gifts outlined in (kjv) Ephesians 4:7-12 and in (kjv) 1st Corinthians 12:28-31.

And these are the "Fivefold Ministry" gifts: the first are **Apostles**, or men and women that establish churches from scratch or build up churches that are failing. They also install ministers into ministerial positions and impart supernatural ministry gifts outlined in (kjv) 1st Corinthians 12:1-11 and (kjv) Romans 1:1-11. They're able to do this because they're equipped with two or three of the fivefold ministry gifts and they have at least two or three of the nine gifts of the Spirit outlined in (kjv) 1st Corinthians 12:1-11. For they have stood at one time or another in one of the nine gifts or all five ministry gifts, or how would they know what a pastor should or shouldn't do (if) they have never been a pastor?

Second, are **Prophets**: a prophet is a person who speaks concerning the future by an anointing or by the Word of Wisdom; which deals with "Foreknowledge" or something that is sure to happen in the future no matter what and this is "Foretelling".

Or he speaks about knowledge of future events that can be changed by obedience or disobedience. (kjv) Jeremiah 38:14-18 and 39:1-8 and Acts 21:8-14. They also speak to individuals or the church for edification, exhortation, and comfort, and this is called "Forth-telling". 1st Corinthians 14:3.

So they will have the Gift of Prophesy and/or Discerning of Spirits, the Gifts of Healing, or the Working of Miracles or one of the other nine gifts of the Spirit operating in their ministry.

Third, are **Teachers**: a teacher is a person who teaches the Word of God supernaturally by an anointing, so they're not like secular school teachers. Therefore, their job is to teach or explain the Word of God with a skill that takes years of study to develop. For they have to show the church what fits and what doesn't fit, or how to rightly divide the Word of Truth. Therefore, they can tell you "How the Bible works and "why" the Bible works. II Timothy 2:15. So they have to know the Word of God forwards and backward, and backward and forwards. And they usually have the gift of the Word of Knowledge or the Word of Wisdom and/or Discerning of Spirits or the Gifts of Healing, or one of the other nine gifts of the Spirit.

Fourth are **Pastors**: a pastor is a person who is a shepherd over a local flock or flocks that are nationally or internationally. For their job is to feed, protect, and watch over the souls of everyone God places under them. (kjv) Acts 20:28 and (kjv) Hebrews 13:17. They usually have the Word of Knowledge and/or the Gifts of Healing or one of the other nine gifts of the Spirit.

And number five is **Evangelists**: an evangelist is a person whose primary goal is to win people to Jesus Christ. So they travel a lot and do more preaching than anything else, and they usually have the Gifts of Healing and/or the Working of Miracles or one of the other nine gifts of the Spirit. Why? Because of all these gifts of the Spirit Are God's **"Supernatural Advertisements"** to draw the masses to Jesus Christ. (kjv) Acts 8:5-8 and 21:8-9. And all of God's ministerial gifts carry with them an anointing. But what is the anointing?

The anointing of God is God on the flesh; doing those things that only God can do. Or it's the **ability** of God or the power of God that will give you the ability to use your gift for Him. Because the anointing of God is literally God's Presence smeared on flesh or a piece of God.

And it is so important that even our Lord and Savior Jesus Christ's **Flesh** had to be anointed by the Father, for He said. "THE SPIRIT OF THE LORD IS UPON ME, BECAUSE HE HATH ANOINTED ME TO **PREACH THE GOSPEL** TO THE POOR; HE HATH SENT ME TO **HEAL** THE BROKEN-HEARTED, TO **PREACH DELIVERANCE** TO THE CAPTIVES, AND RECOVERING OF **SIGHT TO THE BLIND**, TO **SET AT LIBERTY** THEM THAT ARE BRUISED, TO **PREACH THE ACCEPTABLE YEAR** OF THE LORD (or the year of Jubilee)." (kjv) Luke 4:18-19.

And since Jesus couldn't do those things without being anointed, there is no excuse for you, for God will give you the ability to use your gift; for example, I'm writing this book by the anointing or the ability of God. Believe it or not, but this is a small miracle because years ago I could barely write a letter to my family.

But with the anointing and by studying my writing, the ordinary becomes extraordinary by the power of God Almighty! To Jesus be all the glory!

Having then gifts differing according to the grace (or power of God) that is given to us, whether prophecy, let us prophesy according to the proportion of faith. Romans 12:6. But what is faith?

FAITH IS THE SUBSTANCE

The Bible says, "Now faith is the substance of things hoped for, the evidence of things not seen." (kjv) Hebrews 11:1. The word "Substance" the Greek word for "Hupostasis" which means, "The agency or the means, or the instrument by which something was achieved."

Since this is true, faith is the construction worker that brings into reality the blueprint of hope. It is believing the Word of God and then acting on it, or you must act on it by **using** your gift. For faith is the invisible supernatural force that causes things to come into reality.

But most people won't act on faith. Why? Because they're afraid of acting without having any physical proof that their project or idea will work.

But you can't operate in fear and faith at the <u>same</u> time. For one is the reciprocal of the other and the definition of the word "reciprocal" is, "Something existing at opposite ends of each other: like North and South. Or something twisted from its original intent, and then used as evil or inverted of the other."

So, fear is the reciprocal of faith, but it works just like faith because fear is faith twisted or inverted. But the big difference is – it will destroy you and not bless you, for fear steals, kills, and destroys because it's of the devil. St. John 10:10. In other words, faith attracts or pulls you to success, and fear attracts and pulls you to failure.

Like I've said, fear works just like faith because you <u>believe</u> you're going to fail. And, this is why billions of people never use their God-given gifts or only use them a little. Why? Because they're afraid of failure, so they always let others walk on water or do the impossible.

But to be successful, you have to learn to walk on water or do difficult things or impossible things by faith. "For (if) you want what you never had, you have to do what you've never done." Or if you want different - you have to do differently. And you can immediately start doing this by first believing that God is BIGGER than your mistakes, for Jesus helped Peter when he began to sink while trying to walk on water or do the impossible.

(kjv) Matthew 14:22-33. So, don't be afraid to step out of the boat of "Lack" and walk on the sea of "Abundance"!

But how does a person get the faith to do the impossible with? The Bible says, "So then faith cometh by hearing, and hearing by the word of God." (kjv) Romans 10:17. Faith comes by hearing directly from God concerning your gift, or by spending enough time with the promises of God concerning the gift He has placed on your heart until it becomes a part of you like your right arm. Also, you should study everyone in the Bible that has the same gift you have, and this will help you to start believing you can do it. But whether God speaks to you or places something on your heart, you will keep having a sense that you're supposed to be doing something different in life, and it will not go away until you start doing it. And this dissatisfaction will sometimes become stronger or weaker, over time but it will not completely go away because you need to use your gift. (kjv) Nehemiah 2:1-12.

Now faith is the substance for things hoped for. In other words, hope is the blueprint or the picture of what you need to happen, and as I've said faith is the construction workers or the invisible instrument that will bring that blueprint into reality. For faith is a force or a power that causes things to come to you. But the Bible also says, "But wilt thou know, O vain man, that faith without works is dead? Was not Abraham our father justified by works, when he had offered Isaac his son upon the altar? Seest thou How faith wrought (or worked) with his works, and by works was faith made perfect (or complete)?" James 2:20-22. For example, a concrete mix (still in powder form) is useless without adding water to it. And your faith is the same way, so you must act on your faith for it to work for you, or to get results.

This is very important because the essence of power is, "The Ability To Get Results" and this is why (kjv version) Deuteronomy 8:18 quote "But thou shalt remember the Lord thy God: for it is he that giveth thee (by your gifts) Power to get wealth, that he may establish his covenant (or His promises to prosper you) which he sware unto thy fathers, as it is this day." Therefore, faith and your gift are the powers to get money and wealth. But this is still not enough information. Why?

YOUR GIFT HAS TO BE PERFECTED

You see my brother or sister, even if you decide to use the gift that God has given you, you still must perfect it by using it or practicing with it. For it is not what you know – it's what you do with what you know that gets results because knowledge by itself is not enough. You need wisdom, for wisdom is the ability to use knowledge. But how do you get wisdom? You ask for it in faith. (kjv) James 1:5-8.

And this is why it's so important to develop your gift; for example, there is a big difference between growth and development. For growth is automatic because children grow automatically when you feed them.

But development only happens with resistance or by exercising your gift through training; for example, to develop muscles, you have to apply strong resistance by push-ups or by lifting weights, for resistance builds strength.

Your gift is the same way, it must be developed by reading, studying, and even working for someone successful by using the same gift you have. And once you have discovered your gift, you don't immediately quit your job unless God tells you to, for your job is bringing in the money that will help you perfect your gift. Why?

Because when you get off that job you should start working at your new job - which is developing your gift.

Therefore, God will help you by giving you divine "Insight" or the understanding to successfully use your gift to bring in the money and wealth you need and want, for the Bible says," But there is a gift in man: and the inspiration of the Almighty giveth them understanding (or insight.") Job 32:8. In Hebrew, the word insight "inspiration" is, "Neshamah", which means, "To breath on by divine inspiration to give a person intellect."

So, God will help you by giving you insight into how to use your gift most effectively. He will affect your spirit and your mind by speaking to you or by placing thoughts into your spirit or your mind and show you how the thing works.

But this doesn't mean that God will ZAP you with a bolt of lightning! No, this means that He will inspire you by His Written Word, the Holy Spirit, CD's, DVD's, The Internet, or by books on that subject, or by working under wise people and gaining a whole lot of practice through O.J.T (or on the job training). Therefore, in time you will perfect your gift by doing things with it, and by studying it to see what works and what doesn't work for you. And eventually, you will become good at it, and months or years later you will become an expert with it. For in a court of law, an expert witness is anyone that has above average knowledge concerning the subject in question. Why? Because something good made better, is what makes it great. And this is where money and wealth will start to come in, for your gift will make people want to give you these things because your gift will bless their lives.

Believe it or not, but there is no shortage of money and wealth on planet earth. In other words, it goes from person to person and from place to place, but it never leaves the planet, so it's still all here; for example, during 1929, "Great Depression," there were more millionaires created during that time, than any other time in the history of this nation. And to prove this is still true, from 2007 to 2010, during the "Great Recession" more millionaires were created than in previous years. So, during a recession or even a depression, it becomes the best time to prosper. For now, you can get lands, houses, and items for half price or pennies on the dollar, because the people who had "Monopolies" (or cornered the market) on those things are out of business.

And did you know that the Bible talks about prayer at least 500 times and about faith 500 times, but money and wealth 2,000 times? Why? Because quoting the KJV version of the bible (III John 1:2) God said, "Beloved (or talking to you), I wish above all things that thou mayest prosper and be in health, even as thy soul prospereth." Did you notice that he said, "even as thy soul (or your mind, emotions, and will) prospers?" For he knows that to prosper, you must increase your knowledge, wisdom, and understanding to develop your gift. For the old saying is: (if) you don't know anything you can't do anything!

So, let's recap for a moment: you have a gift from God because you were born with it. But it's going to take giving your life completely over to Him through obedience to His written word and obeying his voice when he speaks to you. Because obedience is a sign of integrity. Therefore, you must have the integrity to prosper in the things of God.

Proverbs 11:3. But why? It's simple: your gift can take you, where your <u>character</u> can't keep you. In other words, once God starts blessing you with your gift, if you don't have a godly character you will destroy yourself." But what is character?

Character is doing what's right because it's right when no one can see you, for the Bible says "Blessed (or empowered to prosper) are they that keep judgment (or be fair and honorable, and know the difference between right and wrong), and he that doeth righteousness (or what's right in God's Eyes) at <u>all times</u>." Psalm 106:3.

You see my brother or sister; we are living in an "Honor less Society ". And it's so bad until even when they get caught on tape, they point to the video and say, "That wasn't me! That was my twin!"

We are living in a time of "Situational Ethics", or whatever the situation calls for that's how you play it. In other words, if everyone else is stealing-you steal too!

(Kjv) 1st Corin 15:33 "Be not deceived, evil communications corrupt good manners (character) The word of God states that His people must have good character and whether you can do it and get away with it or not, you don't do it. For you won't do it (if) you want God to prosper you. For doing wrong will gradually catch up with you and **destroy** your success, for the Bible says, "Be sure your sin will find you out (or it will later expose you)." Numbers 32:23 so, always do what's right whether anyone knows about it or can see you.

And since I'm on the subject of character, people can love your gift (but) **not** you. Therefore, don't confuse all the attention you will receive from your gift from people that don't even know you. So, realize that most of them love your gift or what you can do for them and not you.

God wants you to use your gift for His glory and to represent Him in the Earth. Therefore, in the back of this book. there is the prayer on page 89 that will lead you to the path of salvation. Once you repent, which is to confess your sins to God the Almighty and ask God to forgive you of all the wrong that you have done to yourself and others and that you will not continue to sin, but do what is right and pleasing to God. A pastor or minister can help you.

Then pray out loud the prayer on page 74, and you must believe what you are saying. Ask to be baptized in the name of Jesus, read Acts 4:12, and Acts 2:38. Once you have been baptized by immersion in the name of Jesus, ask the Lord to fill you with the Holy Ghost. If you're not born again and filled with the Holy Spirit, and if you are, there is the prayer that you can pray to find out what your gift is, for your gift will either be in the fivefold ministry outlined in Ephesians 4:7-12, or one of the gifts outlined in Romans 12:6-8. Or it will fall under service in the secular realm.

But if you still can't find your gift or "Niche" in this life, there is one more: which is being an entrepreneur or owning your own business.

For God is really into showing you how to become your boss; for example, even in the gifts I've already mentioned, most of them will eventually set you up to be your boss. Why? Because they leave room for creativity.

You see, in times of a bad economy, or in times of a recession you have to become creative, for millions of dollars have been made from creative things coming out of the hearts of men and women; for example, movies, songs, artworks and books. So the Creator says to you through His Word, "I wisdom, (or the ability to use knowledge) dwell with prudence (or increasing your intellect by knowledge, wisdom, and understanding), and (or as a result) find out KNOWLEDGE (or get supernatural insight) of witty inventions (or creative ideas to make money & wealth). "Proverbs 8:12. God uses witty inventions, (but) don't let the word "Invention" throw you off, for the word invention in this scripture means, "A clever idea". For example, a "Patent" for an invention is to help you secure what the "United States Patent and Trademark Office" calls "**Intellectual Property**", so something from your mind that's either technical or mechanical by itself, or has information that shows a person how to do something qualifies for a patent. Therefore, your invention doesn't have to be like inventing the Light Bulb or an MP3 player. No, it can be a clever idea that God will give you to help other people.

And believe it or not, but He has billions of these ideas to give to His children (if) they would fast, pray and seek His Face through studying His Word, and also don't give up until they receive the knowledge of a witty invention. Then once they receive this knowledge, that must perfect the gift until it becomes good enough to produce money and wealth for them; for example, Uzziah, King of Judah prospered by God giving him a witty invention, for the Bible says, "And he sought God (through fasting, prayer, and studying) in the days of Zechariah, who had understanding in the visions of God: and as long as he sought the Lord, God made (or caused) him to prosper (or to increase)." II Chronicles 26:5.

Now in verse 15, in the same chapter, it says, "And he made

in Jerusalem <u>engines</u>, **INVENTED** by cunning (or clever) men, to be on the towers and upon the bulwarks, to shoot arrows and great stones withal. And his name spread far abroad; for he was marvelously helped (by God), till he was strong." II Chronicles 26:15. Now, this was thousands of years ago, but yet God gave this man a witty invention that created an engine! So just think about what he can do for you today! For if you <u>listen</u> to the Spirit of God and be <u>led</u> by him, he will give you witty inventions or something to sell. Romans 8:14, and those inventions will give you money and wealth. Why? Because just praying for money is not enough, for you need something to <u>exchange</u> for money and wealth. In other words, when you <u>solve</u> a problem, now you can receive a **reward,** for money comes from **solving problems**.

Another example of how to receive money & wealth is: when God wants to bless you with either one, He doesn't drop them down from heaven. No, he will give you "**Instruction**" and (if) you act on that instruction, it will produce these things for you; for example, Jesus wanted to bless Peter for letting Him use his boat to preach from, for the Bible says, "Now when He had left speaking, He said unto Simon (or Peter), Launch out into the deep, and let down your <u>nets</u> for a draught." Luke 5:4. But because Peter had been working all night trying to catch fish, and had just cleaned them, he knew that if he obeyed Jesus he would have to clean his nets again. So, he only let down one **old** <u>net</u>, and this half-hearted obedience cost him 50% of his blessing.

For Jesus gave him the instruction, "Let down your NET<u>S</u> for a DRAUGHT (or a whole lot of fish)." Therefore, when God gives you an instruction; obey it 100% and you will receive a 100% blessing. (kjv) Genesis 26:1-14, II Kings 4:1-7, and Matthew 17:24-27.

Now as I've said before, when God gives you a witty invention it's so that you can sell it to people. For there are <u>always</u> people you see every day or that you run into that you can sell something to them, so don't ever be afraid or ashamed to sell things. Why? Because you have been selling yourself to people to get what you needed or wanted ever since you were a baby. In other words, you cried, smiled, and even kicked and screamed until you got what you wanted! And the first secret to being a good salesperson is to believe in your product. Second, sell it for a fair price. And third, always show confidence by looking them in the eye while you're talking to them. And if they have excuses why they can't buy it, you overcome those excuses by showing them why your product is so good **for** them, so they should buy it anyway! For you become a good salesperson by being **bold** and by being **persistent**. For the bottom line of your God-given idea is- you have to sell it; for example, a wise man once said, "If you always have something to sell, you will <u>never</u> be broke."

Now if you don't know God, pray this prayer with me: "Dear God, I'm a sinner, but I believe that Jesus Christ died for my sins and rose from the grave. And on the strength of this, I ask you to forgive me for every sin I've ever committed and I'm sorry for my sins. Lord Jesus, come into my heart and take control of my life. For you said in your Word that if I believe in my heart that you died for my sins and rose from the grave and if I confess you with my mouth by asking you to come into my heart, I will be saved according to (kjv) Romans 10:8-10. I believe Lord Jesus, so I also ask you to fill me with your Holy Spirit. For you said that I could have a heavenly language called speaking in other tongues. So I'm asking you to fill me with your Holy Spirit and I will speak in other tongues by faith in Jesus' Mighty Name according to Luke 11:9-13 and Mark 16:16-18. A-men."

Now begin to worship God by saying "Thank-you Jesus, Thank-you Jesus! Hallelujah, hallelujah, hallelujah! Then <u>start</u> speaking **by faith** any syllables that are not your native tongue. They might sound like gibberish (but) speak them anyway, for if you do this every day along with your regular praying, your speaking in other tongues will become more like a language or more fluent. Acts 2:4. But if you're already a Christian, pray this prayer with me: "Father God, I ask you in Jesus' Mighty Name to give me wisdom on what my gift is and how to use it. For you said in your Word, if any man lacks wisdom, let him ask of God. (kjv) James 1:5. And Lord, give me the courage and strength to develop this gift and to use it to your glory. I ask these things from you and I believe that I have received them in Jesus' Mighty Name. Thank you, my father, thank- you for hearing my prayers and answering them in Jesus' Mighty Name, Amen."

I'm glad you bought this book, for I have prayed that anyone who reads, studies, and puts into practice these teachings, that God would show them their gift and that they would prosper by it, for: A man's gift maketh room for him, and bringeth him before great men. Proverbs 18:16

CHAPTER THREE

How To Find The Perfect Will Of God For Your Life

For sometimes it's hard to find God's Will for a certain situation we're facing even after reading and studying. In other words, we still don't know for sure what God wants us to do, so now we need to hear directly from God in our hearts. But how do you hear from God?

THE WILL

First, let's define what the word "Will" means to understand what the Bible is talking about. The word "Will" in the original Greek writings of the new testament is, "Thelema" which means, "A determination, purpose, inclination, design."

So God's Will; whether good, acceptable, or perfect is something

He has determined, designed, or purposed to happen or allow to happen and He lets it be known by His word. Therefore, God's Will is His written or spoken Word, for words are expressions of a person's intentions or <u>desires</u>; for example, when a wealthy person dies, they leave a "Last Will & Testament" or a legal document telling everyone how they wish their possessions are to be given to family members. And this legal document is **written** in **<u>words</u>**.

The Bible says about God, "In the beginning was the Word, and the Word (or Jesus) was with God, and the Word was God." (kjv) St. John 1:1. Therefore, since God is the Word, His intentions were written down in the Old and New Testaments of the Bible. So, when we want to know for sure what His Will is, all we have to do is read and study His written word. But due to our different lives or circumstances we sometimes find ourselves in, this is easier said than done.

THE GOOD WILL OF GOD

The good Will of God is something that's good in His sight, or what He considers to be something good. For the word "Good" in (kjv) Romans 12:2 in Greek is, "Agathos" which means, "Good in any sense; or benefit."

So the good Will of God is that which can benefit you or that which helps you in some shape or form.

And it's also doing His Will up to a certain point; for example, king Jehu only did the good Will of God to a certain point, for the Bible says, "Thus Jehu destroyed Baal (or satanic worship and the enemies of God) out of Israel. **Howbeit** from the sins of (king) Jeroboam the son of Nebat, who made Israel to sin, Jehu departed

not from after them, to wit, the golden calves (or idols) that were in Beth-el, and that were in Dan.

And the Lord said unto Jehu, because thou hast done well (or good) in executing that which is **right in mine eyes,** and hast done unto the house of Ahab according to all that was in mine heart, thy children of the fourth generation shall sit on the throne of Israel.

But Jehu took **no heed** to walk in the law (or the Word) of the Lord God of Israel with **all** of his heart (or to do the perfect Will of God): for he departed **not** from the sins of Jeroboam, which made Israel to sin (through idol worship)." II Kings 10:28-31. Jehu did a lot of good, but he refused to walk totally in God's Word, even though he would quote the Word of God before he executed God's, Good Will. II Kings 9:24-26. And a lot of Christians are the same way or they quote the Bible, but they only do the portions they like and the rest they ignore.

Now before we get to the "Acceptable and Perfect Wills of God". I want to clearly explain to you that there are blessings for doing the Will of God and there are curses for not doing the Will of God.

BLESSINGS & CURSES

You see my brother or sister; each Will of God carries with it blessings and curses. This is very important because the Perfect Will of God has no curses attached to it. After all, it gives us 100% blessings, or since its 100%, there is literally "no room" for curses. But you still can be in God's Perfect Will and experience suffering. For the Apostle, Paul was in His Perfect Will.

Now before I explain this 100% blessings, I want to define blessings and curses, because a blessing is something spoken over your life or it's done through words; for example, Jacob blessed his sons by telling them their futures by prophecy. Genesis 48:1-22. Also, a blessing means to "Increase" or "Multiply"; for example, a person asked their pastor, "How do you know when you're prospering?" Their pastor said, "When you're increasing". So to be blessed means to be empowered by angels helping you to prosper; you're given the ability to be successful at whatever you do. Psalms 1:1-4 and Genesis 24:34-49. But curses are just the opposite, for they empower you or give you the ability to fail by evil spirits coming into your life. Zechariah 5:1-4. and they're **activated** by words also, because in Deuteronomy 28:15-68 (Kjv). God spoke these curses to Israel and us (if) we disobey His written or spoken word.

Now, these blessings and curses are in effect 24/7, and they start working the minute you obey or disobey God's Word. And to make this point even more clear concerning blessings and curses when dealing with the acceptable, good and Perfect Wills of God.

I will use the parable of "The Sower and The Seed" that Jesus used to explain the different levels of hearing and doing the Word of God, for He said, "And these are they which are sown on good (or productive) ground; such as hear the word, and receive it, and bring forth fruit (or increase), some thirtyfold (or 30%), some sixty (or 60%), and some a hundred (or 100%)." Mark 4:20. This 30%, 60%, and 100% are the acceptable, good, and perfect Wills of God. But there is a serious catch to only doing the Word at 30% or 60%. And that is if you're producing 30% you **still** have 70% failure. If you're producing at 60% you **still** have 40% failure, because these percentages of failures will eventually start to eat up your success; for example, a Christian that only spends 30% of their time praying, studying, and going to church. But they spend the other 70% on the things of this world, like watching movies, playing games, and having fun in the sun. And since they're not that dedicated to the things of God, I can also tell them how much sins and problems there are in their lives – 70%! For the wages of sin is death or the High Price for Low Living is a failure. Failure in their personal lives and their business lives, but this is **acceptable** to God, or they're in His acceptable will. In other words, at least they're saved, study, and go to church **sometimes.**

This is very true for a lot of Christians, but the way God has set life up is, success is according to how much of His Word you do and failure is decided by how much of His word you're not doing.

This is very serious because that 70% that's not done, is like cancer and it will eat at your 30% of success until it destroys it.

That is why Christian's that only believe God for money and wealth (but) not for divine healing, end up spending their hard-earned money and wealth to get back their health, or the 70% eventually ate up the 30%.

But the 100% Christian that does their best to serve God with all of their heart, mind, and body eliminates failure. In other words, like in sports or warfare, the best offense **is** the **best** defense. Or your attack is so overwhelming until it becomes the very thing that protects you.

I'm using this military illustration because the Chinese have an old saying, "Everything is warfare!" And they're right because everything boils down to success or failure in this life. Why? Because you have to fight for everything you need and want, for Jesus said, "The kingdom of heaven suffereth violence, and the violent (or the aggressive) take it (or get the victory) by force." (kjv) Matthew 11:12.

Jesus is referring to the time when Satan and his angels tried to overtake heaven. But Michael and his angels won by force or by being more aggressive. Revelation 12:7-8. The Bible also says, "**Fight** the good **fight of faith**." 1st Timothy 6:12.

Warfare whether spiritually or naturally is a fact of life, for from the cradle to the grave we will have to fight the good fight of faith to survive and be successful. But what is the acceptable will of God?

THE ACCEPTABLE WILL OF GOD

The acceptable Will of God is controversial because what I'm about to teach you, a lot of Christians who are **Super** spiritual will strongly disagree with me.

But I'm going to back it up with three Scriptures, for out of the mouth of two or three witnesses let every word be established. II Corinthians 13:1.

The word "Acceptable" in Greek is, "Euarestos" which means, "Fully agreeable or that which is reasonable, or fits the situation."

Or this is the best you can do according to your level of maturity in God, or you're in a terrible or life-threatening situation. In other words, God understands that you had to do what you had to do to survive; for example, Naaman the Syrian, who was the captain of the army of the king of Syria. He was a leper and a heathen who served other gods, but he was healed of leprosy by faith, under Elisha's ministry, for the Bible said, "And he returned to the man of God, he and all his company, and came, and stood before him: and he said, Behold, now I **know** that there is no God in all the earth, but in Israel: now, therefore, I pray thee (or ask of thee), take a blessing of thy servant. But he (or Elisha) said, as the Lord liveth, before whom I stand, I will receive none. And he urged him to take it, but he refused.

And Naaman said, shall there not then, I pray thee, be given to thy servant two mules' burden (or loaded) of Earth? (he wanted some soil from the land of Israel so that he could keep in contact with the God of Israel when he returned to his land). For **thy** servant will henceforth offer neither burnt offering nor sacrifice unto other gods but unto the Lord.

In this thing (or what he has to do later) the Lord pardon (or forgive) thy servant, that when my master goeth into the house of (the god of) Rimmon to worship there, and he leaneth on my hand, and I **bow** myself in the house of Rimmon: **when** I bow down myself in the house of Rimmon, the Lord pardon thy servant in this **thing**. And he (or Elisha) said unto him, "Go in peace. So he departed from a little way." II Kings 5:15-19.

When Elisha, the man of God or God's Representative said, "Go in peace." He was saying to Naaman that your actions are acceptable to God. For he was in a bad situation because he served a heathen king. And he would be forced to bow down in the house of Rimmon while his king worshipped this false god. But God and Elisha understood his bad situation, for if he refused to bow this would mean certain death to Naaman, so God still considered him to be His servant.

Another example is the "Midwives" for the Israelite women when they were giving birth, for the Bible says, "And he (the king) said when ye do the office of a midwife to the Hebrew women and see them upon the stools; if it is a son, then ye shall kill him: but if it is a daughter, then she shall live. But the midwives feared God, and did **not** as the king of Egypt commanded them, but saved the men children alive.

And the king of Egypt called for the midwives, and said unto them, why have ye done this thing, and have saved the men children alive? And the midwives said unto Pharaoh Because the Hebrew women are not as the Egyptian women; for they are lively, and are delivered (or before) ere the midwives come in unto them (but this was a lie). Therefore, God dealt well with the midwives (or blessed them): and the people multiplied, and waxed very mighty. And it came to pass, because the midwives feared God, that he made them houses." (kjv) Exodus 1:17-21.

Now God is against lying but believe it or not, this is acceptable in a life-threatening situation. For they were given an "Executive Order" from the king to murder all male children at birth and if they refused they and their children would be killed, so God made them houses or He blessed them and their children. He **didn't** tell them to lie, no, but He understood two things: (1) they were heathens (or in some cases baby Christians) and (2) they were in a life and death situation, so they were still in the acceptable Will of God.

The last example is Rahab the harlot, who hid the 2 spies when they came to spy on Jericho, for the Bible says, "And the king of Jericho sent unto Rahab, saying, bring forth the men that are entered into thine house: for they be come to search out all the country. And the woman took the two men, and hid them, and said thus, "There came men unto me, but I wist not whence they were (or I don't know who they were): And it came to pass about the time of shutting of the gate, when it was dark, that the men went out: whither the men went I wot not (or I don't know): pursue after them quickly; for ye shall overtake them. But she had brought them up to the roof of the house, and hid them with the stalks of flax, which she had laid in order upon the roof (or used them to cover the spies)." Joshua 2:1-22. Therefore, she lied, but it saved her life, her family lives and the spies lived and God blessed her, for she is a part of Jesus' Family Tree. For in Matthew 1:1-5, she is called Rachab; who is Rahab the harlot. And Rahab was also used as an example of a person of faith in James 2:25, so she was in the acceptable Will of God.

I remember when I was a rebellious teenager and used to drink wine, get high and gamble with grown men. Why? Because I was a PK or a "Preacher's Kid" and the devil was trying to send me to the abyss "a demandable place" of no return. Anyway, I became so good at shooting dice until I beat some old guys out of their money on the West side of Chicago! For I was hanging out with my older cousin Butch and he had to help me get out of there alive because they were embarrassed and angry that they let a kid beat them at shooting dice, which takes a lot of skill. I also played "Poker", but I would cheat with marked cards, and I lived in Michigan, but I was going again to Chicago to a poker game that night.

So, I was up in my bedroom in the attic marking a deck of cards with an ink pen. But I was concentrating so hard on getting my mark just right, that I didn't hear my dad creeping up on me. He said," What are you doing?!" I quickly put the cards behind my back and said, "Nothing!" He said, "You're marking a deck of cards, aren't you?!" I was busted, so I said," Yeah, I'm marking a deck of cards."

My father used to be a gambler before he became a preacher, so he snatched the cards out of my hand and said, "Give me those cards! I will show you how to mark a deck of cards before you get yourself killed!" So he showed me how to professionally mark a deck of cards and then said to me, "You see son, if you put ink on the cards, all they will have to do is put them under a light, and the light will reflect your mark and you'll be busted." I was shocked! First, because he was a pastor and lived a holy life and I knew this for sure. Because I would hide and spy on him to catch him sinning. For then I could look him in the eye and tell him I didn't want to hear any of that Jesus stuff! But I **never** caught him in sin, and he was the reason why I got saved years later, for I thought that all Christians were hypocrites! The second reason this shocked me so much was, what he showed me was very professional. In other words, you could look at my cards all night under light and still not find my marks.

For that night I went to my poker game and won everyone's money! But they got angry with me and started cussing and accused me of cheating. Suddenly three of them grabbed me and threw me up against a wall! And one of them said, "Hold him! For if I find any marks on these cards, we are going to kill him!!"

He then roughly grabbed a desk lamp and put my cards under them. Then he started studying them one by one and this went on for 5 minutes!

But the more he studied them, the angrier he got until he started cussing and said, "I can't find the marks! Let him go, I guess I was wrong! My bad man!"

I said, "Yeah! I told you I wasn't cheating! You Haters are mad cause I won your money!!" I said this, but I was scared and quickly got out of there!

The cold night air felt really good blowing on my face because I was still alive! And I silently thanked my father for showing me how to mark those cards! But my question to you is, was my father wrong for teaching me that? No, for this was the acceptable Will of

God and he was wise enough to realize it. Now before I move on to the Perfect Will of God, I want to say this. The next time your kids lie to you, see how good they lie to you for it could save their lives in the streets. In other words, if you see them sweating or giving off tell- tell signs, correct them secretly by saying with anger, "At least keep a straight face and looked me in the eye when you're lying to me!" For **until** they get saved and filled with the Holy Spirit, this knowledge could keep them alive in a life or death situation. Why? Because the Bible says about all human beings, "Yea, let God be true, **but every man** a liar." Romans 3:4. So don't be hypocritical, for we have all lied in our lifetime. But what is the Perfect Will of God?

THE PERFECT WILL OF GOD

The perfect Will of God is doing what He wants to be done according to His written or spoken word. It's also what He wants to be done concerning your personal life.

And it only becomes perfect when you do everything, but this is according to who you are and your ability; for example, some pastors have 10,000 members and some will only have 100 members. But numbers don't matter, no, what matters is did **they** do what God told them to do and did they do it to the best of their abilities? If the answer is yes, then they both did the perfect Will of God.

Now we will explore how to be in the perfect Will of God concerning your physical location or your position in the Body of Christ, your money, your mate, your divine protection, and hearing from God. But all of these things are determined by your obedience, for the Bible says, "He that dwelleth (or lives continuously) in the **secret place** of the Most High shall abide under the shadow of the

Almighty." Psalms 91:1. But what is the secret place? The secret place is **obedience** to God's written Word and what He tells you to do personally; for example, He told Samson he couldn't cut his hair, so as long as Samson was obedient, no one could defeat him.

The secret place is also the Perfect Will of God because to be under the shadow of anything. You have to be **close** to that object that's casting the shadow. Therefore, when you're obedient to God, this puts you very close to him.

You see my brother or sister; the good Will of God brings with it a success. The acceptable Will brings with it an acceptable success, and the Perfect Will brings with it a perfect or complete success.

So, when you obey God 100%, you receive 100% blessing or perfect provisions to your spirit, soul, and body. Did you know that God made places before he made people?

THE PERFECT WILL OF GOD GEOGRAPHICALLY

God created the earth (a place) before He created Adam and Eve. And their blessings were based upon a geographical location: The Garden of Eden, for the Bible, says, (Kjv Gen 1:28) "And God blessed them, and God said unto them, be fruitful, and multiply, and replenish the **earth,** and subdue it: and have dominion over the fish of the sea, and over the fowl of the air, and over every living thing that moveth upon the earth." Genesis 1:28. God blesses people but he also will bless a place - then put the people in it. And as long as they stay in that place, they will continue to be blessed. So, God blesses the place and then put the person in it, and everything they will need can be found somewhere in **that place**. To prove this is true, watch what happens after Adam and Eve sinned, "So he

(God) drove out the man (and woman); and he placed at the east of the garden of Eden Cherubim, and a flaming sword which turned every way, to keep the way of the tree of life." Genesis 3:24. You see, God had to kick them out of the garden of Eden because it was still blessed (but) they had just been cursed through disobedience. This is very important, for a lot of Christians are having serious problems because they're out of the Perfect Will of God geographically. They're not in the city, the church, the town, or the position that God called them to, and **nothing** will work right for them until this is straightened out.

For "Places" are very important to God; for example, the children of Israel couldn't enjoy the Perfect Will of God until they came into the **Promise Land**. A land flowing with milk and honey, or everything they needed and wanted. Exodus 13:3-5.

So, when God tells you to go to a certain city or join a certain church, do it. Why? Because your blessings are in that Spot, or just like a Treasure Map: **X** Marks the Spot! And everything you will need is **already** in that place waiting for you, for God made the place **before** He sent you there.

And the devil and wicked people will **always** be trying to get you to move out of your place through disobedience. And if you listen to them you will be cursed just like Adam and Eve. But what is the Perfect Will of God in finding a mate? For **until** they get saved and filled with the Holy Spirit, this knowledge could keep them alive in a life or death situation. Why? Because the Bible says about all human beings, "Yea, let God be true, **but every man** a liar." Romans 3:4. So don't be hypocritical, for we have all lied in our lifetime. But what is the Perfect Will of God?

THE PERFECT MATE

The secret to finding the perfect mate is; go by the written Word of God. Therefore, they will have to be saved and filled with the Holy Spirit and reading, studying, and doing the Word of God to the best of their ability. And just because they **say** they're saved; you should still go by their **fruit** (which takes **time** to show its true character). For Jesus said you would know them and not guess about them by their fruit or what they do. Now we do not judge people, but we have to be "Fruit Inspectors". Matthew 12:33. Plus, he that doeth righteousness **is** righteous or if they're a Christian, they will be doing Christian things. 1st John 3:7. So if you think God sent you that unsaved person, you're **wrong!** Because he will never go against His written Word, for God's Word **is** His Will and His Will **is** His Word.

And they **cannot** be a sinner (or a person who isn't born again) or a worldly Christian, because the Bible says, "Be ye **not unequally** yoked (like two oxen with both of their heads locked in a piece of wood with two holes in it) together with unbelievers: for what fellowship hath righteousness (or with a Christian living right and In Right Standing with God) with unrighteousness (or with a sinner or a worldly Christian that's living wrong and in sin)? and what communion (or partnership) hath light with darkness? And what concord (or harmony or agreement) hath Christ with Belial (or Satan)? or what part hath he that believeth (or is born again) with an infidel (or a person who isn't even saved)?" 2nd Corinthians 6:14-15. But this unequally yoked business goes deeper when you study it out, for if you can be unequally yoked. Then you can be **Equally** yoked or there is a person that is just right for you. In other words, they are equal to you spiritually, mentally, and physically.

And this is why you should use this 5-point test when choosing a mate. But I'm **warning** you that this will not work if you only get 4 out of 5 or 2 out of 5. You must get 5 out of 5 to find the Perfect Will of God concerning your mate.

1. You must be compatible spiritually or you're on the same level. But there are exceptions to this rule because one can teach the other and you two can grow together in the Grace of God.

2. You must be of a compatible character-wise or you have to be able to trust them. For if you can't trust them while you're dating, and you suspect they are cheating on you or you catch them in a few lies. How can you trust them when you get married? Luke 16:10.

You must be compatible emotionally or all past issues that haven't been settled have to be discussed. In other words, you should make sure they're healed emotionally so that you won't have to keep paying for someone else's mistakes. For if they're hurt and refuse to be healed or won't get over it, you will have serious problems because whenever they look at you - they will see them. But how do you know when a person is healed of an emotional scar? A person asked their pastor this same question after being seriously hurt, they said

"How do you know when you're healed?" The pastor said, "When it doesn't hurt anymore."

1. You must be compatible conversation wise or they have to be someone you can talk to. In other words, you should be on the same level mentally or they're at least growing in things that create intelligence. For example, the Bible says,

"A **prudent** wife (or a person who can take care of business) is from the Lord." Proverbs 19:14. So this only pertains to people (male or female) who seek to improve themselves. For if a person has no formal education but read "Self Help" books or have enough **sense** to hire a person to help them. Then they're still prudent, but if they refuse to do anything to improve themselves, they're **NOT** the right one for you.

2. There must be physical, sexual compatibility between you and your mate. Why? Because if they do not meet your standards of physical attraction, believe it or not, the other will not matter as time goes by. For you will be constantly breaking your neck trying to look at what you wanted, and this could lead to adultery and divorce.

3. So, the sexual attraction is important; for example, there was this 80-year-old man who married a woman he found to be very attractive and they had 27 children. She was cooking dinner and he pat her on the behind a few times. So even at 80 years old he still found her to be "Booty-Delicious!" These five conditions will guarantee a successful marriage, for they are the Perfect Will of God for your mate. But what's God's Will concerning your money?

Your $$$

There is an old saying, "There is nothing **funny** when you're messing with my **money!**" This is not only true with people but it's also true with God, for He said, "Will a man (or woman) rob God? Yet ye have robbed me. But ye say Wherein have we robbed thee? In

tithes and **offerings.** Ye are cursed with a (financial) curse: for ye have robbed me, even this whole nation.

"Malachi 3:8-9. This scripture and the scriptures that go with it are the reasons why people have so many problems with money. Because paying tithes and offerings is the **first step** to prosperity.

During this "Global Recession," you constantly see people on TV crying and saying, "I've lost everything! And I can't get a job!" Or "I just got laid off after giving them 25 years of my life!"

But you never hear one of them say, "I'm a faithful tither because every paycheck I get, I give God 10%! And I've lost everything!" Or "I just got laid off and can't find another job anywhere and I've been looking for two years!" You never hear this because (Kjv Malachi 3:10) God said, "Bring ye **all** the tithes into the storehouse (or where you're getting spiritually fed at), that there may be meat (or money & wealth) in **mine house**, and **prove** (or test) me now herewith (or with your faithful tithes and offerings), saith the Lord of host, **if** I will not open you the windows of heaven, and pour you out a blessing, that there shall not be room enough to receive it."

This scripture is a challenge to **you** personally. So God is saying to you, "I want you to **Test Me** with your tithes and offerings. I want you to Test Me and see whether I'm a liar or a Faithful God!" And He's so serious about this issue until this is the only place in the entire Bible where He says, "Test Me!" But what are tithes and offerings?

The tithe is 10% of **any money** that comes to you and the offering is any extra money you want to give to God. The tithe opens up the Windows of heaven and your offerings keep them open over your home for even more blessings.

But the tithe is mandatory, for the Bible says, "And **all** the **tithe** of the land, whether of the seed of the land or of the fruit of the tree, **is** the Lord's; it is holy (or set apart) unto the Lord." And in verse 32 in the same chapter it says, "And concerning the tithe of the herd, or of the flock, even of whatsoever passeth under the rod (or when the shepherds were paying their tithes with sheep, they would have them pass under a rod while counting and the 10th one was set aside for God), the **tenth** (or 10%) shall be holy unto the Lord." Leviticus 27:30-32. So 10¢ on every dollar belongs to the Lord, and if you refuse to tithe He considers it to be robbery. Why? Because it's His money! And Christians who don't tithe, pull up to church every Sunday in stolen cars and wearing stolen clothes!

8% of Christians in America don't tithe (it used to be 88% before the Great Recession), and this is also why 98% of them have serious money problems. Because they are cursed or empowered to fail financially.

No matter how much money they make, they never have enough. And no matter how hard they try to hold on to their money and wealth, they end up losing it anyway to unexpected layoffs, thieves, or natural or man-made disasters.

But no matter what the cause, the bottom line will be lost or decrease. You might be thinking, "But I know some Christians that tithe and **still** lost their jobs!" Yes, they lost their jobs too, **but** I promise you that (if) you keep watching them, they will get another one quicker than anyone else.

For God will move heaven and earth to make sure His Word doesn't fail and this is the scripture they should pray when this happens, for God promised, "And I (God) will rebuke the devourer (or command to stop anything that's trying to destroy your income) for your sakes, and he (or it) shall **not destroy** the fruits of your ground (or your labor); neither shall your vine (nor your business) cast her fruit before the time in the field (or your timing for getting things or doing business will not be off so that you lose things or money), saith the Lord of hosts. And all nations (or people watching) shall call you blessed (or you will still prosper when others are going down the tubes): for ye shall be a delightsome land (or a prosperous person), saith the Lord of hosts.

"Malachi 3:11-12. These scriptures are for the tither that faithfully pays their tithes and layoffs or financial trouble still comes upon them anyway. But they have hope because they can pray this scripture and ask God to rebuke the devourer for their sakes and He will; for example, I was walking with a Minister and a Christian brother who I didn't know. He was very sad and talking to the minister about how the courts were trying to take his inheritance that his grandmother left him when she died.

The minister didn't have an answer for him, so I said to him, "I know we just met, but I know how to solve your problem."

He said, "You do?" I said, "Yes." And then I quoted Malachi 3:11-12 to him. Then I said, "If you were to give me and this minister (for he had been teaching him) tithes of whatever money you still have coming in, as soon as it touches my hands, **this** will reverse the financial curse that's upon you which is causing your problem. I will pray in faith over your tithe and remind God that he said he would rebuke the devourer for your sake." He said, "You know what? I'm going to do that!" So, he split his tithes and started tithing to me and this other minister.

Thirty days later, I asked him how was his situation coming along in the courts. He said, "Brother Winters! When my case came before the judge, he said that their case had no merit, so he refused to hear it and ordered them to give me back my money!" This is great, but tithing is more powerful than just receiving stolen money; for example, a well-known minister took his family to the movies, and while his wife was buying popcorn and he was getting the seats, his daughter disappeared! When the pastor's wife came running to him and told him that his three-year-old daughter was missing! He ran to the lobby and started screaming at the top of his lungs, "Lock the doors!! No one is to leave! Lock the doors!!" An usher walked up to him and said, "Sir! You need to calm down!" He violently pushed the usher away from him and said even **louder,** "Lock the doors! My little daughter is missing!!!"

So, the pastor, his wife, the ushers, and the manager started frantically looking for his little daughter.

Now in the women's bathroom, a woman had his little daughter and said to her, "If you be quiet, I will not hurt you, OK?"

But when she heard all the commotion outside the bathroom door and people calling the little girl's name, she left the little girl and joined the other moviegoers by the door.

When her mother looked in the bathroom again, she found her daughter standing on a toilet seat along with the door shut. So, the manager opened all the doors and this wicked woman slipped out with the crowd.

As the pastor and his family were walking to their car, the pastor's mind went to the scripture found in (Malachi 3:11 Kjv) the word of the Lord spoke to him and said, "I told you that I would **Rebuke The Devourer For Your Sake.**" Then the pastor knew and recognized why his daughter wasn't kidnapped.

So tithes and offerings not only covers financial loss but anything precious to you: like your children. I can prove this is true, for the

Bible says, "And as I may so say, Levi (the priest) also, who receiveth tithes (because of his ministry), paid tithes **IN** Abraham. For he was **yet** (or not yet born) in the loins of his father when Melchisedec met him (or Abraham paid tithes to him)." Hebrews 7:9-10.

This is very interesting because when Abraham paid his tithes, his descendant Levi paid tithes **also**.

Therefore, when we pay our tithes, the blessing of the tithe comes upon our children that are not born and those who are. This is how powerful faithfully paying tithes is!

For once a Christian understands that paying tithes and offerings is the "First Step" to prosperity, they will keep paying them faithfully even when God increases their money and wealth.

But believe it or not, sometimes Christians want to hold back their tithes and offerings when they're making a lot of money; for example, there was this businessman in the church who wanted his business to grow.

So he came to the pastor and said, "I'm paying $150.00 in tithes every two weeks, which comes to $300 a month (but) I need more money to increase my business. Would you pray that God would bless my business?" The pastor said, "Sure", and he prayed for his business.

One year later, his business took off and he became a millionaire. So now his tithes came to $100,000 every two weeks or $200,000 a month.

So, he came to the pastor again and said in an angry voice, "Pastor! Do you know how much money I'm paying in tithes every month to this church?!" The pastor said, "Yes I do." He said, "That's too much money to be giving a church!!"

The pastor said, "If that bothers you so much, I could pray

again and ask God to take you back down to $300 a month!" The businessman said in a hurry, "No that's alright! Please don't do that! I repent for being so selfish and ungrateful in Jesus' Name!" This Christian forgot that God only wanted 10% and he got to keep 90%. And some Christians are also like this when money gets tight, so they start skipping paying their tithes. In other words, they pay tithes sometimes, and sometimes they don't. For they say to themselves, "I can't **afford** to pay tithes this month!" But what they don't know is -that they can't afford **not** to pay tithes!

For your return comes back just like you put it out there. So, if you sometimes pay your tithes, God will **sometimes** pay your bills because whatsoever you sow **that** shall ye also reap.

And before I go on to the next point, I want to say that a lot of ministers teach and preach the last half of Malachi 3:10, the wrong way where it said, "and prove me now herewith, saith the Lord of hosts, if I will not open you the windows of heaven, and pour you out a blessing, that there shall not be room enough to receive it."

The words, "There shall not be room to receive it" is in "Italics" because it's not a part of the original writings. For the translators added these words so that the scripture would make more sense: that's why they're in "Italics".

But this is causing a lot of confusion and frustration in the Body of Christ. Because when billions of Christian tithe and give offerings, they rarely receive so much money back where there is no room to receive it!

This scripture is saying **without** the "Italics", "And pour you out **a** blessing (single and not blessings plural), that not enough." Notice it said, "A blessing and not blessing**s**", for the word "Enough" means, "According to ability; much as sufficient." Or you will receive enough money to pay your bills, and you will always have **enough** for food and shelter. This is what paying tithes will do for you because when others are without a job or about to be foreclosed on God will somehow get you a job or the money to keep you from losing your home. This is what He promises His children, for if He meant what is being taught today, there will be no need to sow a seed (or money) for a big harvest. II Corinthians 9:6-7.

Plus, some Christians don't even know how to tithe in the first place. Why? Because the tithe must always be given by **faith**, and faith is believing God's Word and then acting on it. Or do works that go along with your faith; for example, once you pray for a job; now go out and seek a job by filling out application**s.**

So, you must believe that God will open the Windows of heaven and pour you out a blessing that will be right for you and your family. For without faith it's impossible to please God. Hebrews 11:6.

And, so that you will understand what the word "Impossible" means, it's **impossible** for a man to get pregnant! Therefore, it's impossible to please God with your tithes or anything else without doing it by faith.

Second, the tithe is 10% of any income you get. But **"Tithing"** is done with your **mouth,** or you must pray over your tithe and this is outlined in Deuteronomy 26: 1-4 & 10-15.

But I'm going to write the prayer out for you and cover all the major points. But before you start your prayer, first put the tithes and offerings in an envelope and hold it up in both hands and say, "Dear Heavenly Father, I'm offering up my tithes and offerings unto you in Jesus' Mighty Name." Then set it to the side and say this prayer:

Dear Heavenly Father, I come to you in Jesus' Mighty Name.

Giving you all the glory, all the honor, and all the praise. Giving thanks unto you for all things in Christ Jesus.

I now offer up to you my tithes and offerings in Jesus' Name. And I ask you to look down from heaven and bless me (name the blessing you want; whether spiritual or physical blessing), I asked this from you in Jesus Mighty Name and I believe I received them in Jesus' Mighty Name. For I have kept Your commandments and I have given to the poor. And I rejoice in all the good things you have given me (at this point, start naming all the blessings you have received for the last month. And if you don't have any blessings at all, then rejoice over being alive and going to heaven. So say), I rejoice, I rejoice and I thank you in Jesus' Mighty Name. A-men."

You should do every time you tithe, and if for any reason you can't physically have the money in your hands, write the amount on a piece of paper and put it in the envelope and hold it up to God. But what is the Perfect Will of God concerning divine protection?

DIVINE PROTECTION

What I'm about to teach you is very important, because in these last days you will have to have **divine** protection. But this is not a problem, for when you're in the Perfect Will of God, you're also protected 100% by God. Why?

Because He will have to protect His **Interest**. In other words, if anything happens to you-you will not be able to do His Will in the Earth. For you are the "Star" of His Show and if you die, the show has to be canceled; for example, it's just like your favorite TV show, if the show ends with the star about to die in an explosion or going off a cliff.

But if they show you next week's episode and you see the star drinking coffee or whatever; you know for **sure** they didn't die! And the same is true if God tell you you're going to do this or that next week or years from now, you know in between times you didn't die. This is just a little wisdom and it applies to real life, for you are the star of God's Show.

And this protection is even for your immediate family, for the Bible says, (Kjv Gen 6:13) "And God said unto Noah, "The end of all flesh is come before me; for the Earth is filled with violence through them; and, behold, I will destroy them with the Earth. Make thee an **ark** of gopher wood; rooms shalt thou make in the ark, and shalt pitch it within and without with pitch." Then in verse 22, it says, "Thus **did** Noah; according to **all** that God commanded him (or the perfect will of God), so did he." Genesis 6: 13, 14 & 22. Then in (Kjv Gen 7:1), it says, "And the Lord said unto Noah,

"Come thou and **all thine house** into the ark; for thee have I seen righteous (or in Right Standing) before me in this generation."

God told Noah what to do; which was to build an Ark and he obeyed Him. Remember, obedience puts you in the "Secret Place" of the Most High God.

So the Ark was the Perfect Will of God for Noah and also for his family and instead of the flood killing them, they rode on **top** of the flood.

For when you're in the Perfect Will of God by doing all that He commanded you, you will not only save your life (but) also your children's lives. Why? Because obedience to the written word or the spoken Word of God to you personally, gives you 100% divine protection or it becomes your personal Ark.

You see my brother or sister; we're living in The Last Days and this is why I'm using Noah for example. Jesus said as it was in the days of Noah, so shall it be when I come back. Matthew 24: 36-39.

But how do I know for sure that we're in the last days? The sign is: in Noah's day the whole earth was **filled** with violence. Guess what? The whole earth is filled with violence **Today,** for we are living in the most dangerous generation that ever hit the face of the earth!

And to survive, you will have to **be** (or present tense) in the Perfect Will of God. For this is the **only** protection against crime, random violence, and suicidal terrorists.

So, you have to be doing the Word of God to the best of your ability and you have to be obedient to the Holy Spirit when he speaks inside of your spirit. Why? Because the Bible says that he will show you things to come, both spiritual things and natural things. The scripture says he will guide you into **all truth**. St. John 16:13. And this is the "Saying Word" to you personally from God that I have mentioned in this book.

For in the Greek, there are two definitions of the word "Word".

1. Is Logos or "The Said Word" of God; which is past tense from Genesis to Revelation.

2. Rhema or the "Saying Word" of God; which God uses for miracles; for example, a man said one time to a Minister, "I don't **believe** in miracles!" The minister said, "You will when **you** need one!"

And Rhema is also for personal instructions or wisdom that only pertains to you. In other words, it is a specific word, to a specific person about a specific situation.

But whatever is said to you, it will always be according to the written Word of God and you will have peace in your heart about it. Why? Because the Bible says let the peace of God **rule** in your hearts or if it says you're safe or everything is cool, then it is. But if it says you're wrong or everything is not cool, then it isn't, Colossians 3:15. It's just that simple, because the word "Rule" is the key to this scripture, for you never saw anyone arguing with a 12-inch ruler, have you? No, for rule means you don't get a vote or the Ruler's word is final.

Now concerning the Perfect Will of God, I want to keep this simple: 100% divine protection comes from being in and doing the Will of God completely. For the Bible says, "And the world (or the world's system of doing things) passeth away (or will be destroyed), and the lust thereof: but he that **doeth** the will of God abideth (or will live and be protected) forever." 1st John 2:17.

So, let's recap: there are three Wills of God; acceptable, good, and perfect. And to hear from God, you must first go by the written Word of God. Why? Because if you do not obey what is written in **Black & White,** you will not obey the voice of God when He speaks to your heart.

The Perfect Will of God is geographical, or you have to be in the place or in the position He wants you to be in. I wrote three other books besides this one, and one, in particular is, "A Man's Gift Will Make Room for Him", I combined 3 mini-books into 1, which will help you find your gift or your position. I hope you enjoy this book and purchase one for a friend.

Anyway, the Perfect will of God concerning your money is learning how to faithfully tithe by faith and "Tithing" is done with your mouth. For this is your first step towards prosperity. And the Perfect Will of God concerning your mate is: you have to follow the (5) laws of compatibility.

Last, to be protected, you have to be in and stay in the Perfect Will of God. For 100% divine protection comes from doing exactly what God wants you to do. And you have to live a righteous life like Noah, for you can't live wrong and **expect** right.

Now if you don't know God, pray this prayer with me: "Dear God, I'm a sinner, but I believe that Jesus Christ died for my sins and rose from the grave. And on the strength of this: I ask you to forgive me for every sin I've ever committed and I'm sorry for my sins.

Lord Jesus, come into my heart and take control of my life. For you said in your Word, that if I believe in my heart that you died for my sins and rose from the grave. And if I confess with my mouth by asking you to come into my heart, I will be saved according to Romans 10: 8-10.

I **believe** Lord Jesus, so I ask you to fill me with your Holy Spirit. For you said that I could have a heavenly language called speaking in other tongues. So I'm asking you to fill me with your Holy Spirit and I will speak in other tongues by faith in Jesus' Mighty Name according to Luke 11:9-13 & Mark 16:16-18. A-men."

Now begin to worship God by saying, "Thank-you Jesus, thank-you Jesus! Hallelujah, hallelujah, hallelujah! Then start speaking by faith any syllables (or pieces of words) that are not your native tongue. They might sound like gibberish at first (but) speak them anyway, for if you do this every day along with your regular praying, your other tongues will become more like language or more fluent. Acts 2:4.

But if you're already a Christian, pray this prayer with me: "Father God, I ask you in Jesus' Mighty Name to help me to get in and stay in your Perfect Will.

I also ask you to help me let go of anything that's keeping me out of your Perfect Will. And Lord Once Your

Perfect Will has been revealed to me, give me the courage and strength to walk in your Perfect Will every day. I ask these things from you and I believe that I have received them in Jesus' Mighty Name. Thank you, my Father, thank you for hearing my prayers and answering them in Jesus' Name. A-men."

CHAPTER FOUR

How To Preach Or Teach Great Sermons

You see, just (1) Word from God can change your life forever! And just (1) Word from God can also give you a great sermon. For any Word **from** God is full of power; for example, the Bible says, "God is upholding "All Things" by the "Word" of his power." Hebrews 1:3. This means that all the planets in our universe are suspended in space by God's Word.

Another example is, Peter walked on water by just (1) Word from Jesus. And do you remember what that (1) Word was? Jesus said, "Come". The Bible says, "And when Peter was come down out of the ship, he walked on the water, to go to Jesus." Matthew 14:22-29.

Therefore, don't think this is unscriptural to build a sermon from just (1) Word from God. Why? Because if Jesus gives you a word, you can walk on water. For with just (1) Word from Him, Peter "Walked On" water! But how?

The secret is listening for God's voice, study, and then finding the Scriptures to prove and support your text. For many ministers come up with a sermon based on what they like or what they are presently studying themselves. Or they just preach what others are preaching, you know, David and Goliath, Noah's flood or Daniel and the Lion's Den. But I've found out over the years that this makes you only an average speaker. What's the secret you ask? The secret is to get all your messages directly from God, and then He doesn't have to bless it-it's already blessed! And you will hit a home run every time; for example, I would teach seven days a week,

52 weeks a year and they were all different sermons! How could I do that? Well, there are 773,692 words in the Bible. Therefore, I have 773,692 sermons that I can teach and preach.

PREPARATIONS

First, to be a good speaker, you must pray, you should pray in tongues for 5 to 15 minutes and then with your understanding or regular prayer. Before I would teach, I would first pray in tongues, and then I would pray in my regular prayer. I would say, "Heavenly Father, I come to you in Jesus, Mighty Name. And I give you all the praise and glory in Jesus, Mighty Name (remember, always thank God and praise Him first before asking anything from Him, the Bible says to enter into His courts with praise and thanksgiving, Psalms 100:3-4. Plus, Jesus started His prayer off this way or the Lord's Prayer). I give thanks to you for all things in Christ Jesus. My Father, I ask you what shall I give to your people or what shall I teach your people? I ask these things in Jesus, Mighty Name Amen."

Then I quietly wait to hear from God by him giving me usually just one word that I hear in my spirit or my mind: for example, honor or faith, or obedience. I then take that one or two words and go to my concordance and look up scriptures about that word. Most of the time I know which scriptures to use by the word itself, but there are words such as "Honor" that's a broad subject and I don't know what part to teach about; for example, honor could mean being honest or have integrity, or it could mean having authority, like a judge. So, in cases like this, I write down 3 to 4 Scriptures covering both subjects. And as I'm teaching it the right one will come out, for the Holy Spirit will lead me in the direction of honesty or authority.

Now once I get a word from God, I not only write down the Scriptures on it, but I also study those scriptures. For I'm getting the point or meaning out of them **before** I use them. And sometimes you have to look up words to get their definitions so **you** can understand them and then be able to explain them to others. And sometimes you will even have problems pronouncing them. But I solved this problem by buying the whole Bible on tape and listening to the part I can't pronounce and then practice saying it exactly the way the commentator says it. Why? Because he's trying to make money, so he must get it right.

Once I've done all of this, I meditate on my subject and just think about it or roll it over in my mind and soaking up every point or meaning that God is seeking to get across to us.

I also stop all physical things like TV, working out, or dealing with a lot of people at least two hours before I'm going to teach. This is so that I'm ready in the Spirit before I stand up before people. And this is <u>very</u> important because most ministers believe that they can play basketball or Golf or whatever before they preach and it won't affect their preaching, but it will. For physical things are physical things and spiritual things are spiritual things. So, you have to get your spirit, soul, and body in line with what you're doing. You have to focus on what you're about to teach and you can't be distracted by arguing or playing around before you're about to do the Lord's Work. For I take working for God and handling His Work very seriously. In other words, I don't mix His Business with my business. No, I keep the two separate and His business comes before my business; for example, I've been in the weight pit, and this Christian walks up and says "Hey brother Winters, I need to ask you a question. My mother just died, and I need some Scriptures letting me know that she went to heaven,"

Since this is God's Business, I stopped lifting weights and ministered to the guy by giving him the Scriptures he needs, and I don't start lifting again until I'm finished with God's Business.

Also, when I'm teaching, I always FOLLOW the ANOINTING. I want you to listen to what I'm about to teach you, for this is where most ministers missed out at and as a result don't teach good or produce great messages.

Now to Israel in the Old Testament, the Cloud by day and the Pillar of fire by night represented God's presence or the anointing of God, for the Bible says, "Then a cloud covered the tent of the congregation, and the glory of the Lord filled the tabernacle (or the church). And Moses was not able to enter the tent of the congregation, because the cloud abode thereon, and the glory of the Lord filled the tabernacle (or the presence or power of God was so strong, he couldn't stand up under it). This is where you get being "Slain in the Spirit" or when people fall when hands are laid on them. St. John 18: 3–6 and 1st Kings 8:10-11). And when the cloud was taken up from over the tabernacle, the children of Israel **went onward** in all their journeys: but if the Cloud were not taken up, then they journeyed

<u>not</u> till the day that it was taken up. For the cloud of the Lord was <u>upon</u> the tabernacle by day, and fire was on it by night, in the sight of all the house of Israel, throughout all their journeys."

Exodus 40:34-38. Since the anointing is the presence of God, they were following the anointing. When it moves, they move, with it stopped, they stopped. And this is exactly how a minister is to follow the anointing of God. In other words, if the anointing increases or stays the same while you're on a subject or illustration, then continue in that direction. But if it starts to wane or go down, you're going in a direction that God doesn't want you to go in. But don't let it bother you that you're learning all of this right now, for it is by DOING it or by practicing when getting times to teach. But how does it work?

It works like this, if I'm teaching and using a certain scripture concerning honor based on authority, and the anointing is going down or is lifting off of me, I know that Jesus doesn't want me teaching on authority but honesty. So I start using only the scriptures concerning honesty. You might be thinking," What do you mean by it waning or going down or it seems like its lifting off me?"

You see, the anointing of God is **tangible,** or you can feel it and it comes in different degrees: light, medium, and strong.

For when you're on target, it's medium or strong, and when you're not, it's light or you can't feel it at all.

So, to follow it is to go in the direction it dictates with your scriptures or illustrations; for example, Jesus spoke a lot of parables and a parable is an illustration to explain the **unknown** by the **known.** Therefore, He used words like Seed, Pearls, Tares and Wheat, Leaven, or Yeast. He used words that people could understand to explain Biblical Truths. Therefore, illustrations are exceptionally good for this purpose. So, He will bring to your mind that time you did this or that in your life. Or when you heard this story or that story like the wise Chinese man. Jesus will also bring to your mind Scriptures you have studied in the past to give more understanding to the subject you're teaching on. In other words, He will only use that which you know about. For you should never touch outside of your scope of knowledge, for you will get out there and not know what you're talking about.

TEACH OR PREACH WHAT <u>YOU</u> KNOW

So (if) you teach within the scope of your knowledge, you will always know exactly what you're talking about and can explain things to people. This is another reason why you always go over your subject first before teaching it; for example, I remember when I was learning how to type and after I learned about 6 keys, the book would say, "Practice with those keys, for these are the key's <u>you know</u>." I would do this, but sometimes I would get cocky and try to type keys I didn't know, and I would mess up every time. Why? Because I was going outside of the scope of my knowledge and eventually, I stopped doing this, for it was foolish. I couldn't type keys I didn't know, and a man can't teach or preach what he doesn't know, for he will look and sound ignorant. Another tip is, a human being's attention span is 20 minutes. So, every 20 minutes you say, "Can I get an Amen?!" And they will say, "Amen!" You say this at least two or three times, for then you have their attention again and now you can continue to teach them. And remember, don't ever give them the verse with the chapter, for they will get ahead of you and read it themselves and stop listening to you. And if you ever get to teach and the people are not responding at all or are very depressed, stop teaching and get everyone to stand up and say, "Let's just praise God for 1 minute." Then start saying, "Thank you, Jesus! Thank you, Jesus! I praise you and I give you all the glory! You're a Great God and a Great King, and I praise you in Jesus' Name!" This will lift the heaviness off the people, for the Bible says to put on the garment of praise for the spirit of heaviness or depression. Isaiah 61:1–3. The quickest way to get yourself or people out of depression is to start praising God. For then the <u>presence</u> of God will come down upon them.

As the Lord gives you the text to preach about, write out all your scriptures and even illustrations that the Lord gives you. Or if a current event in the news happens that underscores your subject, use that, for Billy Graham was good at this.

Always make eye contact with the people and don't be afraid of them or get nervous.

What I do is, I say to myself, "I have the knowledge that they DON'T have. So, I don't have to be afraid or feel inferior to them because they need to listen to me! I got what they need!" this works because you feel powerful and strong, and confident. Plus, God gave me this teaching and I know it's going to be good! In other words, it's just like war, I have already won <u>before</u> I fight because I came prepared!

Now if I pray and God doesn't give me anything, I open the floor up for "Questions & Answers." And when they start asking me questions, it will spark teachings and we will cover more than one topic. If I don't have their answer, I wait for a second and see if God quickly gives me the answer right there on the spot. If he doesn't, I say to the people, "I will have to get back to you on that question.

But I promise the next time I see you; I will have your answer." So, I pray and study **until** I get the answer, and this is what made me a good bible teacher.

TIPS FROM EXPERIENCE

The last thing is when the anointing is going down, that God's signal to you it's time to stop. So, wind it up and close, for one of the unintelligent things a minister can do is, keep going when God has stopped using him or her. Then he/she gets on everyone's nerves and the audience does not want to listen to the speaker anymore. I have seen even seasoned ministers do this, but why?

The reason is the anointing is so good (when it's really heavy) until you don't want to let it go! For you're wearing God's suit or His Robe of power and it's better than drugs or sex, so this is why it's sometimes hard to get a Minister to be quiet! There are two more things I forgot: don't ever eat a lot of food before speaking. For your body will be trying to digest all of that food, and it will affect your anointing. And if you're not the guest speaker, they might just give you 15 minutes to speak to honor the fact that you are a minister. But don't ever go beyond your minutes, for older ministers look at this as being disrespectful and probably won't invite you back.

For example, I had to drive my pastor to Chi-Town for he was the guest speaker. We went to a big church and there were 300 people in the segment where he was to speak (this was just one part because the church was so big).

Anyway, I was sitting next to a very old preacher and he said to me, "Son, can you put a quart in a pint?" I said, "Yes Sir".

For what he was saying is, can you put everything you have to say within your allotted 15 minutes? Remember this is very important because the older ministers feel like you're disrespectful if you go over your time limit but if the pastor tells you to continue, then it's all good.

I got up and preached a very good message in 15 minutes, and they loved it (to Jesus be all the glory). When I sat down, the old minister was so impressed he said, "Who did you sit under?! Rev. so in so or Rev. so in so?!" I tried to speak but he was so excited until I couldn't get one-word in. So, I waited until he named off all the big preachers in Chicago. Then I said, "No Sir, I haven't set under any of them or been taught by any of them. I've been taught by **Jesus**!" Or I received my knowledge from Jesus. So never go over your time, and start whining it up 5 minutes before your time is up. And don't say, "The Holy Spirit was all over me and I couldn't stop!" Yes, you could because the Holy Spirit works with us and not apart from us. I want to give you some more tips, for I used to think that when a preacher got loud while he was preaching, it was only the Holy Spirit. This is true sometimes, but it's not all the Holy Spirit or the anointing of God. Some of it is a **skill** in the delivery of words.

There is a thing called "Inflection" of voice, or any change in the tone or the pitch of your voice. Or to signal a question or an exclamation by raising or lowering your voice. In other words, when you want to stress something important, you raise your voice. The Bible says, "Cry aloud, **spare not**, lift up thy <u>voice</u> like a trumpet, and shew my people their transgression, and the house of Jacob their sins." Isaiah 58:1. This doesn't mean that you do this throughout your whole sermon, no, it means on certain points cry loud and spare not, and the more you teach, the better you will be at this. Emphasis is the key to delivering a good heartfelt message. For the more you put your heart into the message or speak with passion, the more people will feel what you're teaching. My dad used to call me a dynamic preacher. Why? Because I would use inflection of voice while I was teaching; for example, a simple thing like saying, "Jesus is Lord!"

This can be dynamic when you say it like this, "Jesus is LORD!!" For now, you have emphasized "IS" and on "LORD".

You see, a good or great speaker is a man that knows the power of words and how to use his words to make his points very clear. Or when to speak in an even tone or a louder tone, also when to pause a little to create suspense in what his next words will be (you should get as many tapes of me teaching as you can).

Because you can learn from them and from other ministers that are successful, especially a minister like Billy Graham.

"For it's not WHAT you say (but) how you say it" that has the greatest effect. I have learned to speak with authority and I learn this from Jesus, for the Bible says, "And it came to pass when Jesus had ended these sayings, the people were astonished at his doctrine (or His Teachings).

For He taught them as one having authority (or knew what He was talking about and had the right to teach it, for He got it from God himself!), And not as the scribes (or writers of the law or lawyers)." Matthew 7:28-29. For when Jesus taught, He spoke with great authority and not like someone speaking about something he just heard. Guess what? I have heard Jesus teach before!

One time I was very depressed, and I went to sleep like this and while sleeping, I heard this voice speaking to me with great authority. It was saying, "You can't give up! You must keep going!

You have to stay in the Word of God!" But how did I know this was Jesus?

I knew because I have <u>never</u> heard anyone speak like this before, for His Words seem like they went right through my being! I mean His Words were so powerful until they not only spoke to me - they spoke through me! This is scriptural, for the Bible says that the Pharisees sent officers to arrest Jesus, "The Pharisees heard that the people murmured such things concerning him, and the Pharisees and the chief priests sent officers to take him." Now after Jesus finished teaching look at what the officers said. "Then came the officers to the chief priests and Pharisees; and they said unto them (or to the officers), Why have ye not brought him? The officers answered, **<u>Never</u> man <u>spake</u> like this man!**" St. John 7:32 & 45-46.

They wouldn't arrest Him, because after hearing Jesus preach, they knew that they had never heard a man speak like this man.

I was the same way, for I have heard some of the best preachers in the world, but never a man spake like this man! And when I woke up, I wasn't depressed anymore, but on fire for God!

Therefore, from that date to this one, I have sought to copy the way Jesus teaches. I speak with authority and with a passion because I want my words to not only move people but also to go right through them. I teach or preach like it's their last day on planet Earth, or like it's my last day on planet Earth!

TEACH OR PREACH LIKE IT'S YOUR LAST DAY

For it could be for example, I remember me and a minister friend of mine were coming out of a store. And I saw this guy leaning up against the wall, so I said to him, "Hey man, we're going to a Bible study do you want to come with us? You need Jesus in your life."

He said, "No I don't need Jesus and I'm not coming to your Bible study. Maybe next time." He then shook his head and walked away.

A week later, I found out that when he left us, he got into a knife fight and was killed. This taught me just how easy it is for people to die and go to hades. So, from that day forward, I teach and preach like it's my audience's last day on planet Earth because it just might be.

And this is why my teaching and preaching is with so much passion and authority. Plus, God gave me what to teach, so they must get it, for it could save their lives and the lives of their loved ones. In other words, what I'm teaching is a matter of **Eternal** life and **Eternal** death, so it's very important. Why? Because there are very serious scriptures that I live by or minister by, for the Bible says, "Son of man, I have made thee a watchman (or minister) unto the house of Israel: therefore hear the word at my mouth, and give them <u>warning</u> from me. When I say unto the wicked (or sinner), Thou shalt surely die; and thou givest him <u>not</u> warning, nor **speakest** (or teach or preach) to warn the wicked from his wicked way, <u>to save his life</u>; the same wicked man shall die in his iniquity; <u>but</u> his blood will I require at thine hand (or I will hold you responsible for his soul). Yet if thou warn the wicked, and he turn not from his wickedness, nor from his wicked way, he shall die in his iniquity (or deeply twisted sin, or sin that he believes is not sin); but thou hast delivered <u>thy soul</u>. Again, when a righteous (or a Christian) man doth turn from his righteousness, and commit iniquity, and I lay a stumbling block (or judgment) before him, he shall die: because thou hast not given him warning, he shall die in his sin, and his righteousness which he hath done (in the past) shall not be remembered; but his blood will I require at thine hand. Nevertheless, if thou warn the righteous man, that the righteous sin not, and he doth not sin, he shall surely live, because he is warned (by you); also thou hast delivered <u>thy</u> <u>soul</u>." Ezekiel 3:17-21.

But you're not responsible for saving the whole world; just the people God put in front of you. Do you now see how serious this is!

This is why in the book of (Isaiah Kjv 58:1) God said, "Cry loud and spare not!" So, once I've taught or preached to people, I'm cool, for now, it's up to them because I <u>did</u> my job. One last point when talking about the anointing of God; which is the power of God smeared on flesh.

CHAPTER FIVE

The Anointing and Sex

There is this phenomenon or strange thing that happens when a minister is strongly anointed while teaching or preaching; for example, one time my Aunt arranged for me to do a "Eulogy" (or a set of words that's usually already in the program) at a funeral in Chicago. I stood on the platform while the casket and audience were below me. I spoke the "Eulogy" and then sat down.

When we arrived at my Aunt's house, she said to me, "Boy, I want to tell you something and don't take it the wrong way. But while you were giving that eulogy, it was like something was on you and it made me want to have sex with you!" When she saw the look on my face, she said, "Now I don't want to have sex with you!" No! I'm just **warning** you that seeing you up there and hearing you speak turned me on! And if it turned me on, I know it turns other women on." I was shocked and didn't know what to say.

A few years later, I got married and was a pastor of a church. One Sunday I preached a powerful message and when I and my wife left the church. I came to my front door, opened it, and then let my wife go in first. Then I went in and closed the door behind me. When I turned around my wife rushed at me and started kissing me! I said, "Hey! What's up with you!!" She said, "I don't know! But we have to go upstairs and have sex right now!!"

Afterward, what my Aunt said years ago came back to me, so I prayed about it and God told me this, "Son, the anointing is My power and men want it bad when they come in contact with it. But women react differently, for it sexually arouses them because it's the greatest power on earth."

Why? Because women are attracted to strength or power, for this is why they like muscles or any form of strength shown by men: like great talent or a lot of money and wealth.

But with men and wanting the anointing is like football; for example, when football players are chasing another football player downfield that's carrying the ball. They chase him as long as he's carrying it.

But the minute he drops it or fumbles it, they **stop** chasing him and start chasing the football! Why? Because they don't want him, they want the football!

But with women, they want the man with the anointing on him and this is **why** a lot of minister's commit adultery. Because when they are ministering to women and they hit on them, they foolishly think that they're so handsome and that's what's causing the sudden interest. **Wrong!**

It's the anointing and this is why when ministering to women you should have your wife present and if you're not married a mother of the church or some sisters from your church present. This will keep you out of sin, Amen? So be **wise** and don't let your good be evil spoken of (kjv) Romans 14:16.

CHAPTER SIX

The Wise Chinese Man

Before I forget, I mentioned on page 3 about using an illustration called the "Wise Chinese Man", but you may not have heard the story before, so I will give it to you to use in one of your sermons.

There was this old wise Chinese man that had a long white beard that he stroked when he was thinking about something serious. He also was wealthy and had a ranch with a lot of horses worth thousands of dollars.

One day the horses broke out and ran away into the mountains, and a friend of his said, "Isn't it terrible that all your horses ran away?" The wise Chinese man stroked his long beard and said, "Well? Maybe".

Later, a ruthless Army general came to his ranch to take by force all his horses to supply his growing Army. But the horses were gone, so he left him in a fit of rage!

Another friend walked up and said, "It was really good that your horses ran away, wasn't it?" The wise Chinese man stroked his long white beard and said, "Well? Maybe."

That same month somebody spotted the horses and his son went and got them. But they needed some of the horses broken, to pull wagons, so his son started breaking the horses.

But one horse threw him off and he broke his leg. A friend of the Chinese man said, "That was bad that your son broke his leg, wasn't it?" He stroked his long beard and said, "Well? Maybe." Three months later the same general came back to his ranch looking for his son to draft him into his Army but because his leg was broken, he couldn't go. And later this general lost the war and everyone with him died. Another friend said, "It was good that your son broke his leg, wasn't it?!"

The **wise** Chinese man smiled real big with a sparkle in his eyes and said, "Well? Maybe!" This is a good story to show us that we don't know what's evil or what's good sometimes, for the Bible says we look through a glass darkly or we don't see the whole picture. 1st Corinthians 13:12.

So always give things time to see whether they're good or evil concerning your life or someone else's life.

A Golden Nugget

This is what I learned watching Billy Graham, who had one of the greatest ministries the world has ever seen. But he said that his ministry was founded on (3) things.

1. Never criticize other ministers or their ministries.
2. Always be honest with handling the money & wealth that comes into your ministry.

3. Never put yourself in a position with the opposite sex that can be questioned; for example, he wouldn't even ride in the same limousine with his secretary or be in an elevator by himself with another woman.

Now all of these Rules he and his ministry followed are according to the Word of God. Why? Because a minister must be "Blameless" in all things. I Timothy 3:1-7; II Timothy 2:20-26 & Titus 1:6-9. For the office of a minister is the "Highest Position" on planet earth. It's higher than a king or a president, or a queen. Because in the Old Testament, prophets set kings in their office. 1st Samuel 16:1-13. Or its God Himself that sets you in office.

So the least pastor with the least church is greater than any king, president, or queen; for example, some news reporters were interviewing Dr. Graham at the height of his success. They said to him, "Dr. Graham, why don't you run for president?' He replied with a smile, "Why should I step Down!"

I could not have typed this excerpt in my book if it wasn't for Willie Jackson, John Yang and Anqua Miller. I had been sick because of having a stroke and could barely do anything, but I knew that I had to share what God placed on my heart to do. I am inserting a teaching on The Blood Of Jesus that was not loaded in the first edition of this book but are available now to read for yourself. There are some important topics I believe need to be discussed. I would like to expound on our supernatural weapons. I want to teach more about The Blood Of Jesus. For now, that the coronavirus has caused a worldwide pandemic and has killed millions and will continue to do so until we get a vaccine that will help to kill the virus.

You see, The Blood Of Jesus is extremely powerful because it can literally Stop death in its path. And it's also a Determent or it stops deadly things "Before" they get started, And, it Prevents The Unexpected in our lives to come on us and Sudden Death; for example, a very successful minister was holding her last meeting, and afterwards everyone was on their way home late at night.

Suddenly a drunk driver came out of nowhere and hit the driver, killing him, his wife and their two daughters instantly! Everyone was devastated, and as the minister was later driving home, she had to pull over because she couldn't see through the tears and couldn't control her weeping! She cried out in a very loud cry, "Lord! Lord! Why??!! I can't understand why You would let this happen to a faithful minister and his family?! The minister could only hear the words of the Lord saying to her "as the writer I believe that there are terrible things that evil people and the devil do that can be stopped or avoided by God's children. They seem like they just came out of the "Blue", but they didn't. For the devil had been planning these murders a long time ago. And the Only Thing that can stop them in advance is The Blood of Jesus. It is the Invisible Divine Hedge or Barrier "That's Already" in place for such an attack. And (if) you By Faith Confess of Plead the Blood of Jesus over yourself, your wife, your children and your business. He will not be able to get in to attack you." After hearing this, I went to the word to study it out, and sure enough there it was in Job 1:9,10 and Psalms 91:10. "There shall no evil "Befall" thee, neither shall any "Plague" (or stroke, or pandemic) come nigh (or close to) dwelling."

Now the word "befall" in the Hebrew means, "Be-Fall or just Happen." Or just came out of the "Blue". Since we now know that Jesus Blood and proof in his Word shows us that He covers these things. We should say this everyday by Faith, "I Plead the Blood, I

Plead the Blood of Jesus Over my body and Over every Aspect of my life. I plead the Blood of Jesus Over every aspect of my Families lives. There is a Blood Line Over all of us in Jesus Mighty Name. And the devil nor evil people can't cross This Blood Line in Jesus Name A-men. I Claimed Them All for the, gospel of Jesus Christ.

I say this every day, and when the Coronavirus hit the whole world, it also hit up against The Blood of Jesus that is protecting me and my family, and it worked in Jesus Name! But this doesn't mean that you won't suffer any hurt or loss. But it does mean you will come out with your life, and God will make up to you any loss or hurt.

HOW TO BIND SATAN

What I'm about to teach you, I received from Jesus Himself. For one day while Rebuking the devil. The Lord said, "Don't say, Satan, I rebuke you! Say this, "Satan, I bind you in the Mighty Name of Jesus! You will Cease from Any Maneuvering against me WHATSOEVER and you WILL NOT maneuver against me WHATSOEVER in Jesus' Mighty Name!"

Now before I began teaching on this, I want you to understand that I've seen this work under extreme conditions; for example, years ago, in prison, I went to the bathroom in the back (this was a dorm setting. And 2 guys were about to engage in bad behavior, and I knew one of them, so I said out loud, "Satan! I Bind you in Jesus' Name! And I command you to cease from trying to bully this guy (and I named his name) in Jesus' Mighty Name!

They stopped immediately and looked confused like they Forgot what they were arguing / fussing about! I said to myself, "Wow!"

Another example that was far more serious, was when I was

inside the walls of Jackson prison. The largest Walled prison in the world at that time, anyway I was teaching on the prison yard in the summer time and there were hundreds of guys on the yard. For each Block held at 300 hundred guys. And I noticed that a 3 on 1 fight was happening in front of me as I was looking over the guy's heads that were listening to me.

The guards didn't see what was happening because of the hundreds of prisoners walking around. They were using Bricks and hitting the guy in the head trying to seriously end his life! It was a terrible fight; the guy's life was about to end as he stumbled trying to find the gate his shirt was the color red before he passed out! And Jesus spoke to me and said, "Take Control of That Situation! So I said, "Satan! I Bind you in the Mighty Name of Jesus! And I command you to Cease from trying to kill this guy in Jesus Mighty Name!" They broke off the attack, and the guy stumbled up to a guard with his shirt wrenched in sweat, stains of his own blood all over himself the guard immediately escorted him off the yard. Now when Jesus taught me this, I didn't even know what the word "Maneuver" meant until I looked it up. And it is a military term that means, "To Set Up For An Attack". Therefore, when you say, "You will Cease from any maneuvering against me WHATSOEVER! This STOPS whatever he was already cooking up on you even Before you woke up this morning!

For we have 16 hours to work with every day, but he has 4 hours. And when you say, "And you WILL NOT maneuver against me whatsoever in Jesus Mighty Name! This stops Future attacks that he will try to set up against you.

Now when you bind Satan, you say out loud with authority or with anger in your voice, and if there are people around you, say it under your breath with the same authority. For he can still hear you because he is a spirit. And sometimes you have to say it more than once or twice when he is bent on doing harm, and in extreme circumstances, you have to say it until the problem or danger is over. Or you don't stop – until he stops So even if it seems like things are cool, you still Watch & Pray. Because there are times when he will, only Leave you for a Season and then start up against you. Like he did with Jesus, Luke 4:13. Jesus also said. "But if I cast out devils by the Spirit of God, then the kingdom of God is come unto you. Or else HOW can one enter into a strongman's house and spoil his goods Except He First Bind the strong man (or the devil) and then he will spoil his house." Matthew 12:28-29. Jesus also said, "And I will give unto you thee the keys (or Revelation Knowledge) of the kingdom of heaven, and WHATSOEVER you BIND ON EARTH shall be BOUND in heaven (or we will back you up) and WHATSOEVER you loose on earth (like money or things stolen from you) shall be loose in heaven. (kjv) "Matthew 16:19. I use this as a weapon against the devil and evil people. And as soon as my feet hit the floor, I bind him, and command him to cease in Jesus in Jesus Mighty Name.

Since we're talking about the spirit of fear, and how someday you could become fearless. One day I was working in the Control Center as a clerk at Michigan Reformatory. This was in 1983 or 1984, it has been so long, I can't give the exact year.

Anyway, after doing all of my work, I was sitting and reading my Bible. And I started hearing men roughly hit my wall. I knew they were engaging, in discourse but this was so common, I kept on reading my Bible. But the argument wouldn't stop and I kept listening for keys to be clinging together as the correction officer ran to the excitement. But no keys! And this was very unusual because the C.O are there in under 60 seconds. (I later found that when the officer got the call, he jumped up and knocked his radio off and was screaming into a dead radio!)

So I got up to see why they were still engaging. When I came on the scene, things were not great. It's good to know Jesus, they had made a circle around these two guys while they were expressing bad behavior toward another guy. A male school teacher was trying to de-escalate what was happening so fast. It was a struggle for the male school teacher to gain some control I notice the guy was slumping down on the wall and was passing out. Then the Compassion of God rose up inside me, and I ran over and got between the guy falling and the guy that was fixing to cause more harm again. And just at that time, the police came and took control over the situation. I went back to my area and my counselor came and, and he said, it was good that you helped that teacher save that guys life. I'm going to put you in for a Wardens Commendation. He did and it helped my record, but I give Jesus' the Glory! For I had no fear, because God had made me fearless.

Printed in the United States
by Baker & Taylor Publisher Services